# Eyes of the Calusa

# Eyes of the Calusa

**Holly Moulder**

**Illustrations by Teri Wilson**

White Pelican Press

ISBN 10: 0-9790405-0-7
ISBN 13: 978-09790405-0-4

Library of Congress Catalog Control Number: 2006939998

Book Production: Tabby House

Cover Design: Carol Tornatore

White Pelican Press
132 Marcella Avenue
Sharpsburg, GA 30277

# Contents

Because they love learning like pirates love plunder,
I dedicate this book to my favorite students:

White Oak Elementary School's Fifth Grade
2004–2005

# Part One

## *Freedom*

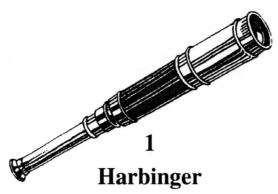

# 1

# Harbinger

*Florida's Golden West Coast, circa 1720*

Sleek and silent in the graying dawn,
the frigate *Devil Ray*,
carrying its wicked company of pirates,
sailed along the virgin shoreline.
The captain,
long golden hair blowing in the breeze,
surveyed the distant beach
through her father's spyglass.
Seeing no signs of the treasure she sought,
she ordered the crew to sail on.
"Head north," commanded Captain Hannah Dunne.
"We'll pass this way again tonight
if our coffle is not already full!"
So the slaver continued on its way,
a sinister specter in the morning mist.

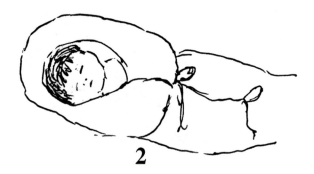

# 2

# Elanu-Y-Mara

Her name was Mara.
She was of the ancient people called Calusa.
They were the fierce people, respected warriors,
builders of shell mounds, canals, vast villages.
She was Calusa.
Her mother told her that the ancient god Hurrican,
god of wind and storm, god of evil,
was very angry on the day of her birth.
For on that day,
he sent treacherous winds and wild waves from the sea
to cover their island.
Her family sought refuge high on the shell mound
where generations of Calusas before her
had found protection from the relentless power of
Hurrican's anger.
The shaman offered sacrifices to Hurrican,
gifts of tobacco, sweet-smelling leaves,
were thrown from high on the temple mound
into the furious sea.
And Mara, though just newborn,
never showed the smallest hint of fear.

In gratitude to the god who spared their lives,
Mother named her Elanu-Y-Mara, which meant
"one who bears the mark of the sea,"
But that is a very long name.
And so she was called just Mara.
And she lived long ago
with her family, by the sea,
in the land the Europeans named
Florida.

# 3

# Calusa Village

The Sun,
ancient orange orb,
slides along the silent sea,
calling out to its sister, Earth,
"A new day is beginning!
Come! Arise!"

*

She lay upon her sleeping mat, listening to
the sounds of early morning:
her father's deep snores
in harmony with
her mother's softer ones,
the gentle sighs of her small sister, Lupa,
as she dreamt of leaping dolphins in the sea.
Mara was comforted by such familiar noises,
the gentle cacophony of her family.

The fronds of her mat rustled as she quietly arose,
picked up her burden basket,
and climbed down the ladder from the hut
to the moist, mossy ground below.

As she made her way through the brush,
she tied back her black hair with a leather thong.
Her hair was very long; it rested in waves on her waist.
She wore a simple shift woven of plant fibers,
made for her by her mother.
At her waist she tied a leather belt
decorated with white and brown shells.

She was tall,
even for the women of her tribe,
but she was very lean, and Mother said
her legs were too long and
her arms too gangly
for her to be called a beauty.

As she walked through the sleeping village
on her way to the beach,
she heard the sounds of other families, like hers,
holding on to the last few moments of rest,
their sleeping sounds
wafted down from above her.

The people's huts were built off the sandy ground,
standing upon poles
the men had hewn of pine and live oaks.
The workers were all resting now,
for soon the village would open its eyes
to the new day dawning.

She hurried down to the ocean, her feet silent and bare,
her arms cool in the early morning dew.
The burden basket she carried
must be filled with enough food for the day.

Her family depended on her
sharp eyes and knowing hands
to gather the choicest clams
the most savory herbs, the sweetest berries.
She would not disappoint them!

She arrived at the beach before any of the other village girls.
and she went quickly to her special place.
Here she knew the clams waited
for her to dig them from the wet sand.
A large shell that had washed up on the beach
was her digging tool,
and her basket was quickly filled with clams,
some as large as her hand.
Mother will be pleased.

The sea oats growing on the dunes
rippled in the morning breeze as
the yellow sun began to warm
the soft white sand.
The air was filled with salty smells of the sea,
the pungent odors of marsh grasses and animal remains
washed onto the shore,
their death providing
nourishment for other creatures.

A hungry band of pelicans
gliding in unison inches above the water,
searched out their morning meal.

Sighting prey,
one left the others, and wheeled skyward,
straight up,
only to turn suddenly toward the water's surface.
Down he dove, shattering smooth sea.
He plunged his head beneath the water
and captured his meal.

Mara stood on the shore and watched
as she did every day.
One by one
the pelicans repeated the ritual,
and, as always, their early morning dance
soaring, diving, and finally crashing into the sea,
made her laugh.

Walking through the dunes,
she searched out the hogplum and the cocoplum.
She found the special holly plant,
its shiny, dark leaves used by mother
to brew her tea.
Cassina,
"the black drink," it was called.

Mother asked for willow root today,
for this plant, she knows, is one that will be needed
if fever should strike,
or if one of the villagers should be in pain.
The people respected her mother
for her knowledge of healing herbs,
and she has taught Mara many of her secrets.

Herbs and tasty leaves,
sea grape and roots,
peppers and papayas
were all found here,
and Mara chose carefully.

Deeper in the dune meadow,
near the base of the scrub pines,
she gathered the goosefoot,
the tasty meadow grass Mother will prepare
with the clams Mara found.
She gathered them all,
her burden basket heavy,
and began to make her way home.

She walked along the trail near the shell wall
that lined the canal beside the village.
The trail lead to the large ceremonial mound,
where the priests offered special gifts to the gods.

On the opposite side of the canal
lay the enormous knoll
built from shells long, long ago.
It was built for the cacique,
the king of the Calusas, great King Caalus.

His home was set high atop that shell mountain.
From there, his royal court
observed the movements of the villagers below.
The commoners worked to
provide the nobility with food, clothing,
and all of the comforts that
the rich and powerful leaders desired.
The great king held
life and death in his hands,
and he was feared by the many nations he ruled.

The great kingdom of Caalus was now only a story
passed from generation to generation,
when stories were told around
the evening fires.

There were but a few Calusas remaining
where there were once as many as the stars in the sky.
Some were carried into slavery by the Europeans, and
some were killed by the terrible diseases the Europeans brought.
Still, those who remain honor the old traditions,
and each generation teaches
the old ways to the new descendents.
In this way,
the Calusas will remain
noble and strong
forever.

Mara followed the trail toward her hut.
At the top of the ceremonial mound
she saw the dark plumes of smoke billowing into the bright sky.
The priests were there already,
preparing the morning sacrifices
that will please the gods of the people.

From behind her
Mara heard the raucous voices of the village men,
calling to each other and joking
as they paddled their cypress canoes toward the shell mound.

There were but a few canoes in the canal that morning,
with several men in each,
paddling swiftly toward the opening in the mound
where high tide had flooded the inside.
Their task, each day,
was to spread a net across that opening,
so that as low tide approached,
all the fish that had been washed in by the currents
could be captured in the net as the waters withdrew
back into the sea.
In this way,
the village got much food for the day.

Mara's brother, Caalus,
named for the long-ago king,
was among those in the canoes.
He traveled to the shell mound twice each day,
to prepare the nets,
and to harvest the catch it provided.

"Lazy girl!"
A grinning Caalus yelled to Mara as his canoe passed by.
"Have you nothing to feed the hungry men
of this village?
We slave all day for lazy ones like you!
What have you got in that basket for me?"
The others in the canoes laughed,
for they knew that Caalus was only teasing her.
She worked harder than them all!

"I have no food for those who pass their days
shouting insults at the women who feed them.
I have nothing in this sack for you,
except perhaps a large piece of driftwood
to use on your head!"

Caalus laughed at his sister,
waved his good-bye,
and continued down the canal with the other young men.

Caalus was a brave hunter and a skilled craftsman.
His masks and figures were intricately and beautifully carved.
He was well-respected in the village
and Mara was proud to be his sister.

Around her neck,
tied with a narrow thread of palm fiber
Mara wore a delicately carved amulet that
her brother made for her.
It was a heron in flight,
long legs tucked beneath willowy wings.

Caalus said that she is like this heron,
graceful and beautiful.
She smiled as she remembered this.
In her heart she knew she would treasure this amulet always.

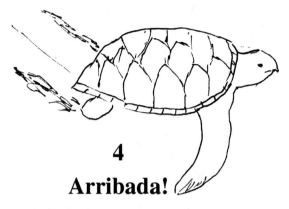

# 4
# Arribada!

"Mara! Mara! Come quickly!"
Mara turned to see her little sister, Lupa,
running to her as fast as she could,
calling as loudly as her little voice would allow.
As she ran, she dragged behind her a favorite toy—
a doll fashioned of palm fronds and sea oats.
Lupa had named her "Pua,"
and she was her constant companion.

"Turtles! Turtles!" she cried.
"They're on the far beach now! Turtles as far as you can see!
Mother has sent us to gather some eggs.
The whole village will be feasting tonight!"

Grabbing her sister's hand,
Mara turned toward the south end of the beach.

Already, many of the village women, baskets in hand,
were hurrying to harvest this feast of good fortune.

Before Mara and Lupa got to the shore,
they saw the vultures
gathering above the cypress trees.
Circling in their hunting dance,
most often harbingers of death,
but today heralds of good news!

The vultures and villagers alike
were eager to consume the warm sea turtle eggs.
The wolves and raccoons,
also fond of this delicacy,
would come after dusk,
ready for their portion of nature's banquet.

Arriving at the beach
Mara discovered that Lupa was not exaggerating
as she sometimes did.
There, stretched before them,
were more turtles than they had ever seen.

Arribada!
The Europeans had called this.

Mother turtles were struggling to make their way
to the dune meadow
where they dug their deep egg chambers.
Scooping moist sand with their wide flippers,
they lay their clutches of eggs.
Sometimes, the mother turtles would lay many, many eggs,
enough to fill her mother's large basket
again and again.

Her neighbors were already at work
harvesting the deep nests.
Mara watched as many turtle mothers,
more than one for each finger on both of her hands,
came out of the sea.
Their carapace was gray, like the clouds at dusk,
and their size was small,
perhaps as long as her arm.

She watched one turtle mother make her way to the dune line,
clumsily, floundering,
unaccustomed to the uneven terrain.
Her weight no longer supported by the sea,
she was heavy and awkward.
Her flippers made short, curving tracks
as they brushed across the sand.
She seemed so tired by her long journey.

She found the place for her nest
snuggled in the sea oats,
safely hidden, she thought,
from all that might harm her eggs.

She began to scoop the sand,
grains flying through the air as she dug.
The mother's leathery round eggs
plopped into the hole she had dug, and
the turtle mother turned to leave.
Without a backwards glance,
she abandoned her children
for the comfort of the sea.

Mara and Lupa watched until her gray shape was hidden
by the breaking waves.
Then, the girls set to work.
They dug through the small mound that marked the nest,
and they continued to scoop out sand
until Mara's arm was deep into the egg chamber,
all the way up to her shoulder.
At last she felt the warmth of the eggs,
and began to bring them up.

Holding several in her hand at a time
she placed them in her mother's basket.
It was quickly filled, and she left the rest
for her neighbors,
or the waiting vultures, or the wolves who would
come to the dune meadow tonight seeking their own feast.

Some of the village men were busy at work harvesting meat
from turtles they had trapped on the dunes.
With sharpened tools in hand,
they were cutting away the carapace and plastron,
exposing the flesh beneath.
The men would take only a few turtles in this way,
only what the villagers could use for food.
The rest of the arribada would return to the sea,
safe at home
until it was nesting time again.

Mara could not bear the sight
of the bloody turtle slaughtering,
so gathering her food,
and her sister,
she made her way back to her home.
Their hands were heavy
with the load of their harvest,
and Lupa's small legs
struggled to keep up with the pace
of Mara's longer ones.

"Mara! Slow down!"
Lupa whined as the girls neared the village.
The older girl turned to wait, and smiled at the sight before her.

Her little sister
pulling her gathering sack behind her,
leaving a trail in the soft sand
like a mother turtle's,
awkwardly, clumsily
coming towards her through the dunes.

# Part Two

*Captivity*

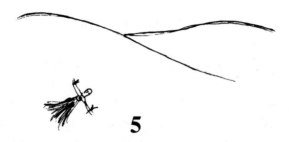

# 5

# Pirates Ashore

The brilliant light of day faded as
the night clouds began to glow,
their gold and amber tendrils
softly caressing the face of the sky.

Tonight the Calusas
would celebrate the generosity of their gods
with prayers and songs.
The priests would light many fires
on the sacred shell mound,
each pyre placed in position to mirror the stars in the sky.
Their fire piles reflect the celestial hunter,
great warrior and guardian of the Calusa people.

As the fires are lit,
the women of the village will lift their voices in unison,
singing praises to the god of the sky,
to the god of the earth,
and to the god of war.

In the Mahoma, the temple,
all the people will dance the ancient dances,
and pray the prayers of tradition.
It would be a fine celebration,
and Mara was filled with the excitement of the evening.

\*

Hannah Dunne recognized the plumes of smoke as soon as she saw them rising into the darkening sky. "Heathen savages are still living there," she muttered. Through her spyglass, she could make out the tribal fire piles built on the tall shell mound.

Captain Dunne hated Indians. Her father had been killed in a skirmish with natives in North Florida. William Dunne had been a pirate, too, capturing Indians and selling them in the slave markets. He stole cargo from seafaring merchants, as well, plundering molasses, rum, gunpowder, and other goods bound for the markets of South Carolina or England.

When he died, Hannah inherited the ship, and the crew was as loyal to her as they had been to her father. The forty pirates aboard the *Devil Ray* had unanimously elected her as their captain. Now, with the help of Mr. Fisher, her father's best friend and first mate, Captain Hannah Dunne patrolled the shores of Florida. She was a slave catcher, seeking out the last of the native Indians, who she would capture and sell at auction in Charles Town, South Carolina, for a nice profit.

"Mr. Fisher," the captain called from her pinnacle post high in the rigging, "ready the skiff to go ashore. Have the crew lower the sails. We don't want the prey catching sight of the hunter." Captain Dunne had learned from her father that the Indians used their smoke signals to warn other villages along the coast when pirate ships appeared.

"Yes, Captain," Mr. Fisher replied. He ordered several of the crew to lower the small ship into the water. Two of the crew, Shay and Shelley, got into the boat and waited for the first officer.

Captain Dunne maneuvered her way down from the crow's nest through the ropes of the tall ship like a spider with a juicy treat trapped in its web. She had grown up aboard this ship, and could climb through the rigging as skillfully as any of the crew. As a child, she had often climbed to the top of the main mast, just to watch the sky and the sea. She was innocent then, and loved her life aboard the *Devil Ray*. She knew her father had made his living as a pirate, but she did not know how much he was hated by the Indians. Until, on her eighteenth birthday, Indians attacked her father and six of his crew who had gone ashore to hunt. The murders were brutal and bloody, and Hannah had vowed never to forgive. Her loathing had made her hard and bitter. Now her sole purpose in life was to capture as many Indians as she could, sell them into slavery, and enjoy the profits of her cruelty.

She smiled wryly at Mr. Fisher. "We have room for one or two more of the savages. Bring me what you can steal quickly and quietly. I do not want to raise the alarm in the village. These are probably some of the last of those foul Calusa, and they were known to be fierce warriors in their day. They also have a reputation for having a strong spirit, which makes them poor slaves, but that will not be our problem. Make haste, now, and be sure to be back before first light."

Climbing into the small skiff, Mr. Fisher gave orders to the men. The boat stole silently through the darkness, barely making a ripple on the smooth sea.

*

Finally, evening had come, and it was time for all the people of the village to make their way to the Mahoma for the celebration.

"Mara, where is your sister?"
Mother asked as they prepared to join the line of villagers
climbing the steep trail to the shell mound.
"She was here, playing by the hut. Did you see her go?"

"Perhaps she is with the other children, Mother.
I saw some running ahead to the Mahoma."
Mara paused and reached for her mother's hand,
"Wait! I remember now!
She was helping me carry home the baskets of eggs,
and she didn't have Pua with her.
She may have gone back to the shore to search for her!"

"Find her, Mara!" her mother said.
"She must not miss this celebration,
and neither should you!
Go quickly!"

Running swiftly, Mara returned to the beach.
The sky's deepening colors warned her
that this day was ending,
and that the celebration would soon begin.
She must hurry!

Scanning the dunes,
Mara spied a small, dark figure digging in the sand.
Lupa!

Seeing Mara, the little girl immediately began to cry.
"I can't find her, Mara! Pua is gone!
I brought her with me to the beach when
we gathered the eggs.
I must have left her here.
Please, please, Mara! We must find her!
She will be so afraid all alone in the night!"

And so, in the deepening evening light,
the two sisters began to search the dune line,
unaware of the danger that was stalking them.
They climbed to the place where the scrub pines grow,
and walked from dune to dune,
searching for Pua

\*

As soon as the skiff came ashore, Mr. Fisher spotted two shadowy
figures moving along the beach. Silently, he signaled for the two
men in the boat to move quietly to either side of the dunes. The
Indian girls, busily digging in the sand, were not aware of the men's
presence in time to save themselves.

\*

Mara heard the unfamiliar noise just as Lupa shrieked her delight at the discovery of her lost toy. "Hush, Lupa!" was all she could utter before the pirates were upon them.

*

Mara was captured first. Her hands were quickly bound with ropes, and a rag was stuffed in her mouth to stifle her screams. She continued to kick and struggle even as Shelley tried to drag her back to the skiff. The younger girl slipped through Shay's grasp and began to run toward the canal. As her pursuer was about to grab hold of her, Lupa tripped and fell, her head striking the solid canal wall. Without a sound, the little one slipped into the dark water. The pirate walked up and down the canal trail, searching for any sign of movement in the water. Sighting none, he shrugged his shoulders, shook his head, and returned to the skiff where Mr. Fisher was ready to head back to the *Devil Ray*.

"Sorry, Mr. Fisher," the pirate mumbled. "She was so fast I could not catch her. She would have been worth a pretty penny at auction."

Mr. Fisher made no comment, but held the lantern lower to get a look at the Indian girl they had captured. "No beauty, that is for sure. But she looks strong enough, and healthy. The captain will be pleased with this one."

*

Bound and gagged, Mara was curled on the floor of the skiff. Her terror and grief were so great that she could not even weep. The horrible men had taken her from her home, her family. And her sister! Lupa! What had become of her little sister? What was to become of her?

She wondered if she was to be a prisoner of these dreaded white-skinned Europeans, those who had brought disease and death to her ancestors. She knew that many of her tribe had been captured and sold as slaves. Her mother had told her the horrible stories of their fate, and had warned her to be watchful, always scanning the horizon for the tall ships that could bring disaster to her people.

35

Slowly, Mara raised her head to look over the side of the small boat. She could still make out the fires burning on the great shell mound. She could smell the smoke from the fragrant offerings the priests were making to the gods. Finally, carried on the gentle sea breeze, she could hear the voices of the village women as they sang the ancient songs of the mighty Calusa.

*

Back on the beach, Pua lay face down on the trail by the canal. In the morning, the tattered doll was found by Caalus as he searched for his sisters. Mara's mother discovered the footprints that the intruders had made in the sand, and she quickly realized that the footprints were not made by the barefoot Calusa, but by the boots of Europeans.

Then, understanding the fate that had befallen her children, she knelt in the water, and wept for her daughters, lost to her forever.

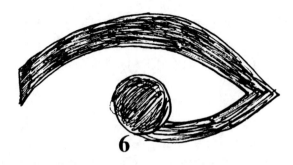

# 6

# Meeting Captain Dunne

Mara's captors handled her roughly as they pulled her from the skiff. They hoisted her up to the waiting hands of the pirates on board the *Devil Ray*. Captain Dunne was waiting on the bridge when Mr. Fisher and his crew brought their captive aboard.

"Good hunting, Mr. Fisher?" the captain asked as the men dragged Mara and threw her at the pirate's feet. The ropes binding her hands and feet were rough and hurt her skin, but Mara refused to cry out.

"Just this one, Captain," he replied. "Not much to look at, but mighty strong. Put up quite a fight. She scratched up Shelley when he tried to tie her up. She would not stop fighting and struggling. It took Shelley and Shay both to get her in the skiff. Anyone who buys her will get plenty of work out of her, if they can ever break that strong spirit of hers. And good luck to them with that!"

Eyeing the new prisoner, the captain instructed the men, "See to it that she causes no problems while she is a guest aboard the *Devil Ray*. Put her below with the others. A few days with no food should weaken that stubborn streak of hers."

"Aye, Captain," the pirate replied, and yanked Mara's arm to lead her away.

"Wait just a minute, Mr. Fisher. What is this?" Captain Dunne pulled back Mara's long black hair, and fingered the beautifully carved bird that she wore around her neck. The woman turned the amulet over in her hand, examining it. Then in one quick movement, she tore it from the Indian's neck. Mara let out a yelp of pain and shock.

Captain Dunne slapped her hard across the face. Mara winced in pain.

"Be quiet, you savage," Captain Dunne scolded as she pocketed the necklace. "You will have no need of this trinket where you are going. We will sell you to some good Christian woman who will beat that heathen idolatry right out of you. Save your worthless soul, she will."

Unable to understand any of the words that the white woman spoke, Mara struggled to comprehend the captain's meaning. But looking into Hannah Dunne's bright blue eyes, she saw the evil that lived there.

Mara's mother had taught her much about the human spirit. The Calusa believe that the soul of each person lives in three places. First, the soul lives in the reflection of the person's face in a clear pool of water. A second place for the soul to live is in a person's shadow. Finally, the most important place is in the center of the person's eye. This third location is where the soul lives, even after death. Looking deep into Captain Dunne's eyes, Mara could see that her soul was angry and cruel. Mara feared her, but she was furious at the woman for taking her necklace, for stealing her from her home, and for having her little sister hurt, maybe even killed. She was determined to show these people the courage of the Calusa tribe. Although she could not speak to them, Mara glared at her captors, the rage on her face made her message clear:

My name is Mara.

You should fear me,

*for I am of the great and noble Calusa.*

The fury in Mara's dark brown eyes did not go unnoticed by Captain Dunne. She laughed at her mockingly. "Yes, I see what you mean about the stubbornness of this one. Courage, too. She will need plenty of that where she is going. Take her below."

# 7

# Samuel

The damp, dank depths of the *Devil Ray*'s lower decks reeked with the odors of filthy bodies, disease, and despair. Mara's first night aboard the slaver was spent listening to the sound of other captives moaning and weeping. One young Indian woman trembled violently as she lay in a corner, vomiting onto the bare floors. An old black man sat propped against a wall, shivering in the dampness, exhausted by the coughing that wracked his thin, bony body. Sheaves of plundered tobacco lay thrown along the walls. Some of the prisoners lay propped against the leaves, trying to find comfort in the cruel surroundings. Most of the captives were people like Mara, Indians from many of the neighboring tribes. All of them suffering and frightened as they were carried far away to places unknown to them, by people who treated them cruelly. Curling her body against the damp wall of the ship, Mara covered her face with her hands, and silently wept, unable to hold back her tears any longer.

Beginning that first morning, and each morning that followed, Mara and the other prisoners were taken up on the deck for hours of brutal work in the relentless sun. She was ordered to feed and care for the crew's flock of chickens kept on board to be slaughtered as food when needed. She collected the "cackle fruit," the name the pirates gave to the chicken eggs they ate daily. She scrubbed the wooden planks of the main deck and forecastle until her hands were raw from the rough brush and cold saltwater. She did not mind the hard work, for it kept her mind off of the terrible fate that had befallen her. Laboring in the sun quieted her thoughts of Lupa and her home.

She learned about sailing by watching the pirates as they went about their chores on the *Devil Ray*. She listened to the strange music that one pirate made by using a large bag made of animal skins. As he squeezed the bag, he blew into a pipe that came out of its side. The noise he made was squeaky and shrill, not soothing like the flutes of her people, but the crew seemed to like it and often sang along as he played.

Mara noticed everything, and slowly began to understand some of the words the crew used as they spoke to each other. She learned "bucket" and "water" and "food." She learned that the large bag of animal skins was called a "bagpipe." She listened to the pirates' songs, and sang along softly to herself, forcing her mouth to make the strange shapes needed to produce the odd words that might help her survive aboard this ship.

Mara was afraid of almost all of the pirates aboard the *Devil Ray*. Shay and Shelley continued to treat her meanly, striking her roughly when she did not complete her task as quickly as they wanted or when she stopped for even the briefest rest. Captain Dunne warned them not to hurt her severely because bruises and scars might lower her value on the auction block in Charles Town, but still they hit her whenever she made the slightest mistake. The other prisoners were treated in the same manner, except for the men, who were kept bound in the hold both day and night. The pirates knew that the young men were strong, and could overtake the ship if they were allowed to roam freely on the decks of the *Devil Ray*. The pirates did not fear the women, however. Only at night were the female prisoners locked in the ship's hold, but they were not tied or chained.

Mara noticed that one of the crew, a black-skinned man called Samuel, kept apart from the rest of the pirates. He did not strike her or any of the other prisoners, and he spoke softly, almost kindly.

One evening, Mara had been allowed some precious time on the deck. She sat quietly, gazing into the darkening sky, hoping to avoid the attention of the crew. Suddenly she felt a presence beside her, and looked up to see Samuel standing next to her. He offered her a slice of the strange fruit he was eating, and Mara accepted it gratefully, examining the piece carefully before tentatively taking a small bite.

"Apple," Samuel said slowly and carefully, pointing to the object in his hand.

"Apple," Mara repeated clumsily, smiling at the strangeness of the word on her tongue. "Apple, apple, apple," she said softly, until she was sure she said it just right.

Samuel smiled his approval. Pointing to himself, he pronounced his name clearly, deliberately sounding out each letter and syllable so that Mara could understand. "Samuel, Samuel," he said.

Mara pointed to her teacher and repeated, "Samuel, Samuel, Samuel." Then, smiling, she pointed to herself and said, "Elanu Y Mara." Now it was time for Samuel to feel awkward as he struggled to pronounce her Calusa name correctly. Smiling, she looked up at him and said, "Mara." Samuel returned her smile, and repeated softly, "Mara."

*

Samuel had been born in Africa. He had lived with his family in a small village, not unlike the Calusa village that had been Mara's home. One day Samuel had been fishing alone in a river near his village, when several men from a neighboring tribe approached him. Before he could yell out, Samuel was bound, gagged, and dragged by the men to a waiting boat. The boat took him to a small cove, where he was moved to a larger ship. The men who captured him were paid well for their efforts, and left the boat to go in search of other young boys who could be sold for such great profit. Samuel was put in chains, and taken deep inside the slave ship.

Samuel's journey from his home in Africa to a plantation somewhere in the Carolinas was interrupted by an encounter with William

Dunne's *Devil Ray*. One overcast morning, as lookouts aboard the slaver had just spotted the Carolina coast, the *Devil Ray* sailed through a camouflage of thick fog to move within striking distance of the poorly armed ship. Spying the pirate frigate, the captain of the slave ship surrendered immediately. Not a shot was fired.

William Dunne instantly took a liking to the young Samuel. As the captain walked the deck of the slaver, surveying the dozens of men chained together awaiting their sale at the Charles Town market, he saw Samuel staring boldly at him. Captain Dunne instantly saw beyond the filthy rags and chains that the young boy wore, straight to the intelligent, fierce spirit that shown through his bright, black eyes.

"Take the rest of them to Sullivans Island, Mr. Fisher," Dunne ordered. "Find Mr. Austin. He will be glad to have this coffle to sell. Tell him this deal has the same terms as all the others. I will expect to see his representative with my money within the next few days."

Captain Dunne paused, and looking at Samuel he added, "Take all of the prisoners except that one. He can make himself useful as my cabin boy. If he cannot do the work, he can be thrown overboard later," William Dunne laughed at his own joke, but Samuel saw an undisguised gleam of cruelty in his eyes. Dunne continued, "If the boy has any sense at all, he will learn to prefer the life of a pirate to the life of a slave. Take him aboard the *Devil Ray*."

Samuel adjusted well to his life aboard the pirate ship. He learned by watching, for he had sharp eyes and sure hands. He became adept at climbing the rigging, and his excellent vision made him a favorite lookout. His bright intelligence and his willingness to help made him a favorite among the crew.

The captain's young daughter, Hannah, took it upon herself to teach him English, which William found both amusing and ridiculous. "He does not need to know how to talk, Hannah. He will never be anything more than just another pirate on this ship. He needs to know only enough words to follow my orders."

Undaunted by her father's chiding, Hannah continued the lessons, and after many months Samuel was speaking and understanding the language as well as any man on board the ship. When Hannah tried to teach him to read, however, her father put a stop to it. "Your game with this African has gone on long enough. There is no use in teaching him to read. If he has time to read, then he has more time to work. There will be no discussion about this matter."

So Samuel's reading lessons came to an abrupt halt, but a strange bond had developed between the African and the captain's daughter that was not exactly friendship, but was instead a kind of mutual respect that would continue well into their adulthood.

\*

After that first night on the deck of the *Devil Ray*, Mara's English lessons continued. Whenever Samuel had an opportunity during the day or in the evening, he would talk to Mara, teaching her new words and reviewing those he had already taught her. Captain Dunne knew of the lessons, but did not stop them. Instead she told Samuel, "Continue teaching her if you want. Being able to understand the language of her new masters will only raise her price on the auction block."

Mara learned to sing the songs that she heard the pirates singing, just to practice the sounds. Her favorite, a song she would later discover was sung to attract young men to sign on as crew members aboard pirate ships, had these words:

*Sing a song of sixpence*
*Pocket full of rye,*
*Four and twenty blackbirds*
*Baked in a pie;*
*When the pie was opened,*
*The birds began to sing;*
*Now wasn't that a tasty gift*
*To set before the king!*

Slowly, very slowly, Mara was learning this new language, the language that would be such an important part of her new life.

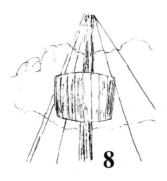

# 8

# A Pirate's Fate

The day of the storm dawned ominously. Clouds in the colors of newly formed bruises stained the horizon. Blood-red streaks of sunlight slashed the sky like open wounds. The air was heavy and still. Mara knew that the scarlet sky was a bad omen for those who travel on the sea, and she could tell that the crew was made anxious by the weather, too.

One man in particular, Mr. Leon, seemed especially nervous that morning. He was a tall, skinny man, with a large scar over his right eye, and the little finger from his left hand was missing. The remains of last night's supper, crusty and brown, stained his broken yellow teeth. Mr. Leon stayed as far away from the prisoners as he could. He rarely spoke to them, and was never in charge of finding tasks for them to do. He avoided looking into Mara's eyes, but once she caught him staring at her when he thought she was not paying attention to him. When she turned towards him, he quickly looked away, but not before Mara caught a glimpse of the terror in his eyes. His shadow, trembling and quivering in the heat of the sun, shook with the fear of his frightened soul. Mr. Leon was terrified of the Calusa.

"Captain, you cannot trust these heathen," Mara had overheard him say that morning. "These Calusa will kill a good Christian man in seconds. Some say that they are cannibals that eat the flesh of their enemies. Look at the way that girl looks at you, like she can see straight through you. She would cut your heart out in a second if she had the chance. And now, bad weather is churning up out there and it is all because of her and her evil, idol-worshipping soul. Get her off this boat, Captain, before she causes the death of us all."

The captain became very angry. "Now listen to me, you fool! She is precious cargo on this ship. She is worth more to me than anything or anyone, including you with all your superstitious nonsense. Mind you keep an eye on her and if we do have some bad seas ahead, make sure she and the others are safely below. Do you understand, Mr. Leon?"

"Yes, Captain," he grumbled as he stalked off.

The weather worsened as the day went on. The seas turned to a deep emerald green that mirrored the angry sky. The wind chopped at the tops of the swells, and waves spat white foam onto the deck. By nightfall, the rain began to splatter on the ship, like small pebbles hitting the wood. Soon the full force of the storm began to hammer the *Devil Ray*. The winds screamed through the sails, and even the seasoned pirates were frightened.

"Lower the sails!" Mr. Fisher ordered above the tumult of the storm. Shelley and Shay moved quickly to follow his commands, but already a tear could be seen in the topsail.

As the thunder rolled across the deck and the lightening lit the sky in great bursts of fire, Mara realized that she must do something to save her own life and the lives of those onboard.

*If only I could speak to my ancestors they would tell me what to do. They would understand what must be done to silence the fierce gods of the sky who harass us tonight.*

Mara stood silently for a minute, and then understood what had to be done. Remembering the ceremonies she had seen performed many times by the temple shaman, Mara returned to the hold for sheaves of tobacco. Calusa priests offered tobacco to the god of the earth and wind to quiet his anger. She had heard the song that the women sang to calm the ancient spirits, and tonight she would sing as loudly as they.

Mara looked at the swirling black clouds filling the sky, and at the waves breaking over the ship. Picking up an armload of the green leaves, she moved unsteadily toward the rope ladder that led to the highest point of the ship, the crow's nest. Mara had watched the crew climb this rope many times, and she knew that she could do it, too.

The offering of tobacco should be made at the high point on the shell mound, but this place, precariously perched in the fury of wind and rain, would surely please the angry god so determined to take the lives of all aboard the ship. Mara climbed hand over hand, slowly at first but then more quickly as she gained confidence.

As she moved through the sodden ropes, Mara heard Shelley yell, "Come down here, you crazy girl! You are going to get yourself killed!"

Mara continued to climb, and everyone gathered below to watch. She struggled to grip the rigging tightly as she made her way to the crow's nest. The gales twisted and turned the ropes as sheets of rain pummeled her body. Carefully she pulled herself into the small basket at the top of the ship's main mast. Mara grabbed the leaves from the belt of her shift where she had secured them, and holding them tightly in her fists, she raised her hands to the stormy skies.

As loudly as she could, Mara sang the song of the women, begging the gods of this tempest to accept the offering. Singing the familiar melody over and over, she threw the tobacco into the air, and watched as the wind lifted it higher and higher into the blackened sky until she could see it no more.

As Mara's offering disappeared, the wind faded and the thunder quieted. The sea, though still rough, lost its wildness. The storm had finally passed.

Suddenly, Mara felt herself being lifted from the crow's nest. "What are you doing?" Hannah Dunne screamed in her face. "What good would you be to me if you fell from here and killed yourself?"

With one arm placed firmly around Mara's waist, Captain Dunne carefully carried her down through the rigging.

On the deck below Mara could see the terrified faces of pirates and prisoners as they watched in amazement. Mr. Leon was yelling something at Mara, and snatches of his screams reached her ears as they continued their climb down to safety. Just as they finally reached the deck, a loud crack was heard, and the crew looked up to see the main mast fall from the sky, striking the deck of the forecastle. Mr. Leon used the distraction to let loose his anger and fear at Mara.

"Idolater! Demon!" he shrieked. "Worshipper of pagan gods! The devil himself is at your beck and call! You must die!"

Mr. Leon lunged at Mara then, his eyes wide with terror. He hoisted her in his arms and hurled her over the side of the *Devil Ray* into the churning waters below. The sea quickly covered her as waves pulled at her, dragging her into the dark depths. Mara struggled to the surface for a breath of air, but was quickly sucked back into the watery darkness. She knew that she was lost.

Suddenly, Mara felt two strong hands grab at her. She felt herself being lifted to the water's surface where she gratefully swallowed huge gulps of air. Her rescuer held her tightly as he swam through the waves back to the ship. The hands of pirates and prisoners alike worked together to lift them from the sea to the safety of the *Devil Ray*.

Samuel had risked his life to save Mara's.

"Thank you, Samuel," Mara gasped as she collapsed on the deck. A blanket was tucked around her shoulders, but still she shivered, more from terror than from the cold ocean water.

Captain Dunne was speaking to Samuel. "My father was correct when he told me of your bravery and loyalty, Samuel. You have earned the respect of all aboard this ship, and you shall be rewarded well for your actions."

"Bring Mr. Leon to me," the captain ordered. Shelley and Shay dragged him across the deck, his hands and feet bound with chains.

Captain Dunne began, "I told you that this girl was one of the most valuable items on the ship. Certainly she is of more value than you, a weak, stupid coward. You attempted to defraud the *Devil Ray* and her crew of the value of this girl, this merchandise that would bring much wealth. A vote of the crew will decide your fate."

It was unanimous. Mr. Leon was found guilty, and he was sentenced to marooning. At the pronouncement of his fate, the pitiful pirate wept and pleaded for mercy, but Captain Dunne would not renege on her decision.

"May your god be as merciful and faithful to you as Mara's. Perhaps he could be persuaded to save your miserable soul, but I would consider that a waste of his time."

At dawn the next morning, Mara watched as Mr. Leon was loaded onto the jolly boat. Shelley handed him a bottle of beer, some bread, and his cutlass. "Do not look so sad, Mr. Leon," Shelley taunted him, "just think of this as a chance to become the governor of your very own island!"

Several of the men on deck laughed at Shelley's joke, while two of the crew manned the oars and rowed the little boat toward the island that could be seen far off on the horizon. Mr. Leon's shoulders slumped in despair as he rode to his fate, his last hope gone.

"Set a course for New Providence, Mr. Fisher," ordered Captain Dunne. "We will repair the damage to the *Devil Ray* and take on the supplies we need to get us to Charles Town."

"Yes, Captain," Mr. Fisher answered, and the *Devil Ray* began its turn into the golds and yellows of the rising sun.

# 9
# A Pirate Paradise

One night, while they practiced English, Samuel told Mara that when a pirate slept, he did not dream that he died and went to heaven. Instead, a pirate's dream always took him on a wonderful journey back to the tropical island of New Providence. Once she saw the beautiful place, rising like an emerald from the depths of an azure ocean, Mara thought she understood why. The gentle breezes, the lush green forests, and the white sandy beaches combined to make this land the loveliest Mara had ever seen. It was not just its beauty that made New Providence so attractive to pirates, however; it was the lack of law and order on the island that made this place a pirate paradise.

*

As a child, Captain Dunne had visited New Providence many times with her father. She had accompanied him through the taverns and pubs of the rowdy town, listening as her father went about swapping sea stories with ship captains and making deals with their quartermasters. She had watched as the crew traded in their hard-earned cash for tankards of rum and ale. She had learned to dodge the drunken fist fighters cavorting in the dust and dirt of the narrow streets. She had even heard the pirates yell their terrible curses at each other, and discovered that she had a knack for using the new words they had taught her, much to her father's dismay. And it was in New Providence one night that Hannah met Edward Teach, the infamous pirate Blackbeard.

Captain William Dunne, with daughter Hannah in tow, had just entered one of the noisy, smoke-filled taverns common in the back alleys of the town. As her father made his way to a group of men sitting in the rear of the bar, Hannah briefly lost her grip on her father's hand. In an instant he had disappeared in the crowd.

Frantically scanning the room for her father, Hannah's eyes landed on a group of men huddled around a table in a nearby corner. In the dim lantern light, she could see that the group was intently listening to one man, a large black-headed man with a long, wiry beard. When the man stopped speaking long enough to take a gulp from his cup, his fierce, dark eyes met Hannah's frightened ones. The young girl turned away, but the pirate, looking for a little sport, called out to her.

"Are you lost, little one?" the pirate asked mockingly. "Come over here and sign on with Edward Teach's crew. Work aboard the *Queen Anne's Revenge* with us, and you will see riches beyond your little girl dreams!"

As the other pirates at the table laughed, Hannah turned to run from the room. Suddenly she was stopped by a strong familiar arm around her shoulders. "Answer him," her father whispered in her ear. "Look him square in the eye and tell him you sail on the *Devil Ray*. Never show your fear to any man, pirate or king."

Looking up into her father's serious face, Hannah found the courage to speak. "My name is Hannah Dunne. I have no need to work on your ship for I sail on my father's ship, the *Devil Ray*. Good evening to you, Captain." Taking her father's hand, Hannah turned to leave as the men in the room shouted their approval at the brave little girl's answer.

"Wait," yelled Captain Teach. "I would like to share a drink with the courageous young lady and her father, if you please. You answer well for one so young. Come join my crew and me for a cup of this fine rum!"

So that night Hannah and her father sat down at the table and listened to the tales of Blackbeard and his crew until the streets of

New Providence were awash with the light of a new day. It had been a night that Hannah would never forget.

*

William Dunne taught Hannah that although New Providence may look like paradise, it was really just a hole where thieves went to hide. During their many voyages to the island, her father had shown her the remote atolls and cays where the *Devil Ray* could be safely hidden until repairs were completed or supplies taken aboard. For in this pirate haven, he said, no property was safe from thieving hands.

She had listened well to her father, and so at high tide on the first day of their stay, Hannah Dunne directed the careening of the *Devil Ray* onto the shore of a small cay out of sight of the main island of New Providence. She needed to keep her ship and its cargo protected from the prying eyes of marauding pirates who would like nothing better than to add to their own booty by stealing the treasures of their comrades.

"Steer her toward the shore," Captain Dunne shouted. "Go straight ahead to the beach and lay anchor. At low tide, she'll settle gently right here in the sand. Then the crew can scrape her hull and make the necessary repairs to the mast and sails. Mr. Fisher, tell the quartermaster to go into the town to get the supplies we need. You go with him to make the arrangements to acquire the wood for the mast. We will stay here as long as necessary to get the *Devil Ray* fitted for the voyage to Charles Town.

"Be sure to tell the crew that their hard work will be rewarded with plenty of time ashore for drinking and carousing. Just see to it that the work gets done first!"

Mr. Fisher and the quartermaster climbed aboard the jolly boat that was lowered down into the gentle waves. Although their hideout seemed isolated and protected from the gangs of pirates inhabiting New Providence, the town was actually just a short row through a narrow straight that wound through the tiny cays and atolls encircling the large island. It seemed that Captain Dunne had indeed picked the perfect hiding place.

Shelley and Shay were put in charge of moving the prisoners along with the rest of the *Devil Ray*'s cargo from the ship to a large cave that the ocean had carved in the rocks near the shore. With its mouth resting well above the tide line, the cave would serve as an excellent storage room for Captain Dunne's treasure.

Mara was overjoyed to feel sand beneath her feet for the first time in many weeks. It felt warm and soft, in sharp contrast to the cold dampness of the *Devil Ray*'s hold. The cave, though dark even in broad daylight, made a more comfortable prison because it was dry and not as cramped as their previous quarters.

As months passed, the crew and their prisoners adjusted to the daily routine of life on the little island. Every day more repairs were made to the *Devil Ray*. The wood for the top mast was ordered and readied for fitting aboard the ship. All hands helped scrape barnacles off the ship's hull, prisoners working side by side in the tropical sunshine with their pirate captors. By trading some of the tobacco and other goods aboard the *Devil Ray*, the quartermaster was able to provide the workers with a variety of the fruit and vegetables that he found in New Providence. There were beef cattle and wild hogs to be slaughtered and roasted on huge fires, so everyone ate well. One night each week, Captain Dunne sent half of the crew to New Providence where they drank rum in the local taverns. The rest of the crew stayed behind, serving as lookouts and guarding the prisoners.

One day, not long before the *Devil Ray* would be ready to leave the island, Shay brought in the remains of the topsail that had been shredded in the storm. Handing Mara a bone needle, he taught her how to make a new garment for herself. The shift she had been wearing since her capture had been ripped when Mr. Leon had thrown her overboard. Captain Dunne had ordered that she be dressed appropriately for the auction in Charles Town.

Mara set to work on her dress, pulling strands from the heavy material to thread through the needle, and then binding the dress together. She found a large clam shell one morning on the beach, and Shelley allowed her to sharpen it on rocks near the cave entrance. She used the makeshift tool to cut away any extra fabric or threads, and soon the dress started to take shape.

Whenever she could, Mara searched the shoreline for seashells that bore the telltale sign of a moon snail attack. Moon snails, or shark eyes as they are called by some tribes, are small, round, gray-striped mollusks that use their peculiar arm-like limb to drill a tiny, perfectly round hole in other sea creatures with shells. After the hole is drilled in the shell, moon snails feast on the soft body of their prey, hidden inside.

Mara searched out the shells with the moon snail holes so that she could link them together with dried seaweed. In this way, she made a belt for herself that was admired by the other prisoners and even the pirates themselves.

"You are very clever, Mara," a smiling Samuel told her one evening as he was admiring her handiwork. Mara smiled at the compliment. He had continued to teach her English during their stay in New Providence, and Mara was now able to understand much that was said to her. She still found speaking the strange tongue difficult, but she kept practicing. Samuel was an excellent teacher. He was also Mara's only friend.

Six months quickly passed, and the time had come for the *Devil Ray* to set sail again on the open ocean. The ship's new mast stood tall against the clear blue sky, its sails snapped in the warm tropical breeze, and its sleek hull begged to be let loose in the gentle currents of the Caribbean Sea. Shelley and Shay brought the prisoners out of their cave and loaded them onto the ship. At high tide, the anchor was raised, and the *Devil Ray* began the last leg of its voyage, the trip that would end in the slave markets of Charles Town, South Carolina.

## 10

# Charles Town Market

The *Devil Ray* slid through the black waters of the inlet near the Charles Town harbor just after dusk. A lantern waved twice on the shore of Sullivans Island to signal Captain Dunne that it was safe to unload her cargo. Mr. Fisher ordered the skiff to be loaded with the remaining sheaves of stolen tobacco, while Samuel moved the prisoners into the small jolly boat. Tobacco and prisoners were to be taken ashore and exchanged for cash in a secret meeting between Hannah Dunne and the Charles Town merchant Donald Austin, her father's partner from long ago. Under cover of darkness through the marsh and maritime forest, the stolen goods would be carried by wagon to Charles Town's busy market place.

Among the prisoners only Mara knew what was going to happen there. Samuel had already told her what horrors lay before her at the slave auction. He thought it best that Mara knew what would take place so that she could try to prepare herself. She was sick with terror, but determined not to show her fear to the others. Since the day of the storm, her companions had regarded her with respect, and valued her leadership. Mara would not disappoint them. Her courage had protected her that day in the crow's nest, and she knew that it would help her now.

Samuel was the first to jump from the jolly boat when it reached the mangrove trees that hid Mr. Austin's wagon. He hauled the boat in as close to the shore as he could, and waited as Captain Dunne climbed through the enormous prop roots of the mangroves to where Mr. Austin waited. Mara watched as their transaction was quickly completed. Several of Mr. Austin's slaves had accompanied him on this evening's mission, and they hastily loaded the tobacco from the skiff onto a wagon. Next, they came for the human cargo. They bound the prisoners' hands with coarse ropes, and gestured for them to climb into the wagon. It was awkward climbing through the mass of roots, and Samuel came to help them. When he lifted Mara into the wagon with the others, he whispered, "Be careful, Mara. Be brave. Show them the courage of the Calusas." He patted her hand, and when she looked at his face, Mara could see tears on his cheeks. She thanked him for his friendship, and watched as he climbed back into the skiff. Then, without meeting her eyes, one of Austin's slaves tied Mara's feet tightly so that she was unable to move. This was not necessary. Even if she could free herself, where would she go?

As the wagon pulled away down the darkened trail, Mara gazed up into the night sky. She studied the stars that formed the Great Hunter, protector of her people, and she hoped with all her heart that his eyes were on her this night.

Mara was startled to hear Captain Dunne call out, "Wait! Hold the wagon!" Coming to where Mara was seated with her back propped against rough wood planks, she untied a piece of twine that was hanging around her neck. Carefully she pressed the necklace into Mara's bound hands. "I will always remember your bravery in the storm, Mara," she said quietly. "This trinket has no value to me, but it may mean something to you. Keep it. I have no use for it." With those words, she turned and walked back to the skiff where Samuel waited for her.

Looking into her clenched hands Mara saw her heron, the amulet that Caalus had carved so long ago. Pressing it to her heart, she felt tears pricking at the backs of her eyes. As she turned her face toward the night sky, she prayed to the Great Hunter and whatever other gods might be listening, asking them to keep her safe on this fearful journey.

The wagon carried its weary cargo through the black night to the outskirts of the city called Charles Town. Dawn was just breaking over the river as they came to a stop behind a large wooden building. The prisoners' legs were finally freed of the heavy ropes, but their hands remained bound together as Austin's slaves pulled each person from the wagon. They were led into a long narrow room where bales of straw had been thrown helter-skelter on the floor. Resting against the straw were black-skinned men, women, and children, hands bound, eyes desolate in the dim light of a single lantern. The prisoners from the *Devil Ray* sat along the walls with them, exhausted by their journey, terrified of what this day would hold.

In spite of her fear Mara found that she must have slept for a short time, because she was suddenly jarred awake by a man's loud yell. "Get up! Get up! The auction is going to start in an hour! We have to get you all ready for the buyers out there. Now, get up!"

He and his crew dragged them to their feet, and sorted the men and the women into two lines. He gave each woman and child an ugly woven sheath to put on, and Mara grimaced with embarrassment as she pulled hers over her head. The children, their eyes wide with fear, clung to their mothers. First, the men were bound with heavy chains around their necks and hands. Their legs were shackled. Then the women were also bound, but with coarse, heavy rope that cut into their necks and wrists. To the beat of the auction's drum, the long, sad queue was led into the yard where a crowd of white planters waited to make their bids.

Potential buyers inspected each of them. Teeth were checked, eyes and hair were examined, muscles were prodded and poked. The auction began with the young men, known as "black ivory" because of the high price they would bring. Bids were made, purchases were sealed, and families were broken apart forever. Children were ripped screaming from their mother's arms as they were sold to owners whose plantations were miles and miles apart. The cries of the children punctuated the calls of the auctioneers and the yells of the eager buyers. It was a horrible scene, and Mara was sick with fear as her turn came to climb the platform stairs.

The rope was cut from her hands and neck as she stood before the crowd of excited bidders. She could hear her heart pounding in her ears as her knees trembled. Mara closed her eyes and clutched the amulet around her neck, willing herself to have courage. She felt a tear roll down her face, but she wiped it away before anyone could see. The auctioneer spoke to her gruffly, "Turn around, girl. Let them have a look at you." Mara pretended not to understand, and the auctioneer pushed her roughly around the platform, showing her off to the bidders. Keeping her chin high, Mara stared into the eyes of each man who offered a price, defying them to try to purchase her.

"That one is too spirited to tame," one man announced. Several others grunted in agreement.

"But gentlemen," offered the auctioneer. "Look at her hands and arms. She's done hard work before. She's a smart one, too, and brave. Why to hear that privateer Hannah Dunne tell it, she saved the *Devil Ray* from one nasty squall. Climbed the rigging and prayed to her gods, she did, and Hannah said that right then and there the storm quieted down. Now, who cannot use a little of that kind of magic when the sun is parching the rice fields and the ground is in need of a good soaking? She might be worth a fortune to you then!" Many in the crowd grumbled at that, and some even backed away in fear.

*Perhaps no one will want me!* Mara's heart leaped with hope, but her joy was short-lived.

"Twenty pounds," a man yelled from the back of the crowd.

"Sold to Stanley Hall!" the auctioneer hollered, relieved and pleased with the price.

As Mr. Robert Stanley made his way through the crowd to pay for his purchase, Mara was loaded onto the back of a waiting wagon, and hauled away from the auction house. She did not look back.

*

The sun beat down relentlessly on the South Carolina low country as Stanley Hall's overseer Stephen drove the wagon across rough, sandy roads. Mara marveled at the immense live oak trees with their outstretched limbs that shaded the trails. She breathed in the fragrances of this land, the strong scent of unfamiliar flowers along the side of the road mixing with the pungent odors of marshland. The deep green leaves of magnolia trees filtered the harsh sunlight while their milky blossoms spread a thick perfume through the humid air. Much of this new land seemed familiar to Mara, like the palmetto palms and the busy buzzing of mosquitoes. Although this familiarity was comforting in some ways, it also made her very homesick for her home by the sea.

The trip from the Charles Town market took nearly all afternoon, and Stephen passed the time telling her what he thought Mara needed to know about the owners and their family. "Robert and Anne Stanley are good white people. They treat us fairly and feed us real well. Of course, I get the best treatment because I am the overseer, which means I tell you what you will be doing each day."

He paused briefly and then continued, his voice low and serious, "You do what I tell you, work hard, and you will get along just fine. I have my ways of dealing with slaves who are lazy or disobedient." Mara stole a glance at Stephen's face, and understood that his last words were meant to be a threat.

He went on talking about the master and his family. "The Stanleys have two children, a girl and a boy. The girl, Miss Grace, knows a lot about growing things. She is the one that got us started raising the indigo, the finest in Carolina. Mister Louis, the little boy, is always getting into one scrap or another, playing with the little black children running around the plantation.

"Now listen, Mara. The Stanleys are good Christian people. Do not be talking about any of that Obadiah witchcraft like you did on the *Devil Ray*. Mistress Stanley will not allow any of that around her home. She will be giving you a new name, too. We all have names from the Bible. She got my name, Stephen, from this man in the Bible who was real brave even though he got himself killed. I am real proud of my name. Do not worry. Mistress Stanley will pick out a fine name for you.

"Mistress Stanley is sickly, so we are careful not to upset her. Master Stanley is away a lot on business, and Miss Grace and I mostly take care of things while he is gone. Stanley Hall is a good place to live. Just do what you are supposed to do and you will get along all right."

Although she was confused and frightened, Mara responded simply, "Yes, Stephen," and they continued on their journey.

The day was almost over when Mara caught her first glimpse of Stanley Hall. The trail widened, the magnolia trees parted, and there it stood. Mara had never seen such a large building, built on two floors with huge windows peering out at her from each of its four walls. Its brick sides were the color of muddy clay, but the window trims and doors were painted the color of fair weather clouds. Just beyond the house she could see wisps of vapor rising above the surface of a great river, which she would later learn is called the Cooper River.

A silvery heron lazily slid through the mist, heading for its evening nesting place. Far to the side were the rice fields, deserted now that the day was ending. Stephen steered the wagon along a narrow path that led past a group of small buildings tucked out of sight behind the main house.

A black-skinned woman was pulling laundry from a rope line, folding it, and placing it in a basket. She looked down at the ground as the wagon rolled by, unwilling to meet Mara's gaze. Stephen paused in front of the outbuildings long enough for a man to come unload the other cargo Mr. Stanley had purchased today. Barrels of flour, and bags of sugar and tea were carried into the little white cottage, and Stephen and Mara continued on their way.

Mara was the last bit of chattel to be unloaded. Stephen drove the wagon through a stand of live oaks to a cluster of huts hidden back in a thicket of tall thin trees and low hanging vines. The huts reminded Mara of her Calusa village. They stood off the ground on long poles and their roofs were thatched with palmetto fronds. Each hut had one large window framed by shutters that could be closed in bad weather. There were as many huts as Mara had fingers on her hand, but many more people were gathered outside around pits that held cooking fires. Dark-skinned women were stirring large pots over the smoky fires, while laughing children ran in and out between the huts. Tired black men trudged slowly home from the fields, their backs bent with exhaustion from the day's grueling work.

"Get out here," Stephen ordered, and he turned to speak to one of the women gathered around the cooking fires. "Sarah! I have a new girl for you. Find her a place to sleep. She will be working the indigo tomorrow. Have her ready."

A plump, light-skinned woman smiled up at me. "Come with me, child, and I will take care of you. What is your name, girl?"

"I am Mara," she answered haltingly as she followed Sarah into a dimly lit shack. The furnishings were sparse and shabby, but Sarah's warm smile made her feel welcome. "You will sleep there for now," she said, and pointed to an empty corner by the window. She pulled a threadbare quilt from a pallet on the other side of the tiny room, and laid it on the floor for Mara.

Suddenly a young boy flew into the tiny room, all arms and legs and noise. "Timothy!" Sarah hollered at him. "Slow down now, boy, and come meet Mara. She is going to be staying with us for a while."

"Hello, Mara!" Timothy's smile was as genuine and warm as his mother's. He was a big boy, but probably about the same age as Lupa. Thinking about her little sister brought sadness to Mara's eyes that Sarah saw immediately.

"Come, child," she said gently. "Sit down on the stool and let me fix you some bread and beans. You have had a long, tiring day, and you must be hungry. Timothy, go fetch Mara some cool water."

As Timothy hurried out of the hut to do as he had been told, he nearly ran straight into the biggest man Mara had ever seen. His skin was the color of a cormorant's wing. He had huge arms and legs, and he filled the little room with his presence. Mara was very tall, but she felt dwarfed by this man's height.

"Abraham, come meet Mara," said Sarah. "Stephen left her with me. She will be working the indigo tomorrow, and I am supposed to get her ready. Mara, this is Abraham."

Mara smiled shyly at Abraham, and was rewarded with a wide smile that brightened up the entire room. "Welcome, Mara!" he said, and she was certain that his booming voice could be heard all the way to the main house.

Her life at Stanley Hall had begun. Deep in her heart Mara wondered, *Will I ever leave?*

# 11

# Indigo

The morning light of the new day spread gently over the slave quarters of Stanley Hall. Roused from her slumber by the morning routine of Sarah preparing breakfast for the family, Mara made her way to the outhouse. She could see the morning mist as it rolled off the river meandering past the main house on its way to Charles Town harbor. Crows cawed and squirrels chirred at her from their perches in the pine trees. Spanish moss dripped with the humidity of a low country morning.

After relieving herself into a bucket, Mara carried the liquid to a large wooden vat. The slaves' urine was used to prepare the blue indigo dye for which Stanley Hall was renowned. Sarah told Mara last night that one of her chores each day would be to collect the urine from the slave quarters and carry it in buckets to the indigo house.

After a breakfast of bread and beans left from the night before, Mara went to each of the slave houses and collected the waste. Hauling a heavy wooden bucket in each hand, she tried to walk quickly so that she could finish and get away from the horrible stuff. But when she moved too fast, the liquid splashed up on her legs and stained her skirt. It was a terrible job, and the pungent stink of the urine made her sick to her stomach. Sarah had assured her that, with time, she would grow accustomed to the odor. Mara did not think that getting used to such a horrible smell was something that she wanted to do.

After carrying the last of her load to the indigo workers, Mara made her way back to Sarah's hut. Through the open door, she could hear Sarah talking to Timothy. "What is wrong, boy? Tell your mama what is ailing you this morning."

Walking into the room, Mara could see that Timothy was lying on his pallet, curled into a tight ball, his tear-streaked face turned toward his mother. "Mama, my head hurts something awful, and I feel like I am burning up." Timothy's voice was quiet, and he looked so weak, lying on the tattered blanket that served as his bed. Could this be the same little boy who had run into the hut last night? Mara crossed the room, and laid her hand on his forehead. It felt very warm.

"Sarah," she said, "In my village, my mother was the healer. She knew all of the plants and herbs that could be used to cure the illnesses of my people. She was teaching these things to me." Mara paused for a moment, thinking how far away her mother was now. It seemed to Mara that she had been away from her home forever.

"Mother taught me to use willow root for fever. She showed me how to make a tea from it. Would you like for me to make some for Timothy?"

Sarah smiled at her, gratitude shining in her eyes. "Please, Mara, I would be so thankful."

Taking a basket, Mara made her way down to the river where she knew she could find everything that she needed to make the healing tea. After gathering the necessary ingredients, she hurried back to the hut where she brewed the willow root and other herbs in a pot of water. When it cooled, she gave a cup to Timothy. He sipped the tea and laid his head down on the blanket. In moments, he was gently sleeping.

"Thank you, Mara," Sarah said quietly so she would not wake her son. "We must leave him now and get you to work in the indigo fields. Stephen will be angry if you are late, and you do not need to feel his lash on your first day. Come now and I will show you the way."

Taking a glass jar of water and some bread for her noontime meal, Mara followed Sarah around the rice paddies to the higher ground where the indigo was grown. Many old women and children were already there, carefully cutting the indigo so that the leaves' powdery coating did not rub off. This work had to be done quickly, otherwise the hot Carolina sun would dry the leaves before they could be taken to the soaking vats.

Mara made the trip to the vats many times that first day. The indigo cuttings were laid in the large, cypress tubs that were as wide as she was tall, and twice as long. If she stepped into the vat, the smelly liquid would probably come up to her shoulders. But fortunately, that was one job she would not have to do.

After the indigo leaves had steeped in the vats for half a day, another slave who was known as "the Indigo Maker" would drain the liquid into a tub that was called "the beater." Mara watched as the men took long poles with bottomless buckets on the ends and quickly stirred, or beat, the indigo until it became foamy on top. Oil was sprinkled on the foam, and then the liquid was closely examined to see if it was ready for the lime water that would cause the liquid to finally turn the indigo blue color. Soon granules began to form in the water, and bits of coarse purple sand settled into the bottom of the tub.

This "Indigo Mud," as the sandy material was called, was stored in linen bags and hung to dry until it became a paste. Then it was spread out on wide boards with a large wooden paddle for further drying. Finally, the dried powder was cut into bricks, packed in wooden barrels, and shipped down the river to the Charles Town markets.

Stanley Hall's indigo was very famous. Miss Grace Stanley had devised this method for making the cakes of dye, and had shared her ideas with other local planters. Now, all of the plantations in the low country used her technique, and were becoming rich because of it.

Later that afternoon, when the sun had finished its brutal baking of the Carolina fields, Mara returned to Sarah's hut. There she found a very different Timothy! Instead of lying quietly on his mat, he was up and about, running around the hut, and begging to go play with the other boys.

"Please, Mama," he begged. "Please let me go play with Mister Louis! Mara's tea made me feel so much better, and Mister Louis and I have built a raft that we are going to float in the river today. We have been working on it for days and days, and today we are supposed to try it out. Please, Mama!"

Smiling at her son, Sarah finally acquiesced. "All right, you may go. But beware of those snakes and other critters down there in the marsh. This is the time of year for them to be especially nervous about intruders around their homes. Keep a close watch and a sharp ear!"

Like a prisoner released from his cell, Timothy bolted through the door. Sarah laughed, and continued with her work. "He and Mister Louis have been the best of friends since they were tiny, tiny boys. They share more adventures and get into more trouble than any two children should! Here, Mara, take this bit of meat out to the pot. You can help me with the cooking.

"As you settle into your life at Stanley Hall, Mara, you will find there are good, kind people here. Abraham, Timothy, and I will be your family now. We can never replace the family you had in that far away place, but we will love you all the same. To be trapped in the bonds of slavery is terrible, to be sure, but to let the master own your heart and soul and mind would be unbearable."

Touching Mara's forehead, Sarah looked deep into her eyes and spoke gently. "They cannot own you here," she whispered. Then putting her warm hand over Mara's heart, she said, "and they cannot own you here." She smiled then, and continued with her work.

Deep inside her heart, Mara felt the warm truth of Sarah's words.

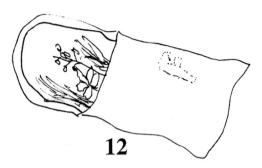

# 12

# Mistress Stanley

"Sarah, I do not know what to do this time." Mara heard the pretty young lady say as she drew closer. "Mother is complaining about a terrible aching in her head, and she has been warm with fever since yesterday morning. We have sent to Charles Town for the doctor, but he is too busy to come right now. I thought maybe you would have some healing herbs that I could try. I know the people here trust you to take care of them when they are sick." Her eyes pleaded with Sarah for help, and Mara could see the concern for her mother written in the worried lines of her face.

"Miss Grace," Sarah replied, "I am not certain that I have anything that could help Mistress Stanley. I would be happy to make a poultice for her if you would like, but that is really only good for stomach ailments and such."

Sarah saw Mara listening close by. "Come here child," she beckoned to her, "and meet Miss Grace. This is Mara, ma'am."

Miss Grace turned to look at Mara. Smiling at her she said, "Welcome, Mara. My father told me that he had purchased a new slave. He told me he was very impressed with the courage you displayed at the market. He thinks your strength of spirit will be an asset to us here at Stanley Hall."

Although it was not proper to look into the faces of the masters, Mara could not resist a peek at Miss Grace's brown eyes. They were warm and shining, full of love and intelligence—a reflection of Miss Grace's soul. Mara was comforted by the gentleness that she saw.

"I am sorry that the mistress is ill," Mara said sincerely. "In my village, my mother taught me to use the root of the willow tree to care for sicknesses like the one you describe. Would you like for me to prepare a tea for her?"

When Miss Grace hesitated, Sarah spoke up. "Please, Miss Grace. Yesterday my own Timothy was sick with the fever, and Mara brewed a tea for him that fixed him up in no time. By the end of the afternoon, he was begging me to let him go down to the river to play with Mr. Louis. I have never seen any of my remedies work that fast!"

Smiling, Miss Grace replied, "All right, Sarah, if you approve of her treatment, then I cannot really object, can I? Please gather the plants that you will need, Mara, and come to the rear of the house. Our cook will help you with any preparations that you require. But please hurry. Mother is really feeling very poorly."

Miss Grace hurried back to the house, and Mara went into the hut to get her gathering sack. She ran to the woods behind the slave quarters, searching for willow and other healing roots. Filling her sack, she hurried to the kitchen door of the main house.

A chubby, dark-skinned woman opened the door and immediately began chattering at Mara. "You must be the new girl Miss Grace told me about. My name is Eve, and I am the cook. Come on in, and tell me what you need. The mistress is very ill this time, and nothing we do for her seems to help. She said that her head feels like it is about to burst wide open and her skin is burning hot. Just tell me what to do, and I will help you." The poor woman wrung her hands, fretting over the condition of her mistress.

Within a few minutes, Mara had a soothing tea and an herb poultice ready for Mistress Stanley. Miss Grace came in to the kitchen, and Mara told her how to use the herbs that she had brought to care for her mother. Mara waited while Miss Grace took the medicine upstairs. Still distraught, the cook continued to babble about her mistress.

"She is such a good Christian woman," Eve whined. "So kind to all of us, and so thoughtful. Why, for Christmas last year, she gave me a fine pair of gloves that she did not need anymore. They sure were pretty. She takes care of all of us like she really wants what is best for us. Building that chapel for us to have Bible teachings, giving us Sunday afternoons to do whatever we want. I do not suppose there is another mistress in all of Charles Town who treats her people any better. You be thankful you came here, girl, instead of going to one of those plantations where the slaves are mistreated.

"Mister Stanley, too, is a fair man. Now he is gone away from home a lot because he has businesses here and there, but he makes sure this plantation is running like it is supposed to. Miss Grace sees to that. She sure does have a good head on her shoulders to be such a young girl like that. Yes, the Stanleys are one fine family."

Eve continued chattering until Miss Grace reappeared in the kitchen, her eyes gleaming with joy and relief. "Mara, your medicine has already begun to work! Mother says she feels so much better! You are a wonder! My father was right when he said that you would be an asset to our home. Thank you so much!" And with that, Miss Grace hugged her so hard Mara could barely breathe. Her heart was bursting with pride at the praise Miss Grace had given.

"Mother would like to meet you, Mara, to thank you. Please come with me. We will only stay for a moment because she is still weak and I do not want to tire her further."

Mara had never been in the Stanley's house before, and she could not stop gawking at the riches she glimpsed as she was led through the formal dining room, parlor, and entry way. Beautiful paintings filled the walls, and Miss Grace smiled as Mara stared. "I can see that you like my paintings, Mara. I enjoy creating them for my family."

Mara followed Miss Grace up a tall, winding staircase to a large bedroom. She suddenly felt shy as she entered Mistress

Stanley's room. It was a wonderful place, with a grand view of the river through its huge glass-paned windows. Mistress Stanley was sitting up in an enormous carved bed, holding the cup of tea that Mara had prepared for her.

"So you are Mara," the older lady said kindly. The girl nodded her head and took a few tentative steps forward.

"Yes, ma'am," Mara replied, her eyes lowered to the floor. "I am so glad that you are feeling better."

"Come here, Mara, so I can see you better. I would like to thank you for making this wonderful tea for me. It is delicious, and I believe it has relieved my fever. I hope that you will make it for me again if I should need it." She was smiling at her now, and in her eyes Mara could see the sweet soul of a wise and gentle woman.

Again Mara found herself wondering how people as kind as Miss Grace and Mistress Stanley could choose to hold her at Stanley Hall against her will, to hold her here as a slave.

Mara pondered this thought constantly as she worked day after day in the indigo fields of the plantation, harvesting the crop that would make her owners still wealthier. More than anything else, Mara longed to go home.

# 13
# Sunday Morning

### On being brought from Africa to America

TWAS mercy brought me from my *Pagan* land,
  Taught my benighted soul to understand
  That there's a God, that there's a *Saviour* too:
  Once I redemption neither sought nor knew,
  Some view our sable race with scornful eye,
    "Their colour is a diabolic die."
  Remember, *Christians, Negroes,* black as *Cain,*
    May be refin'd, and join th' angelic train

—Phillis Wheatley, a young slave girl and renowned poet, 1753–1784

The next morning, Sarah woke Mara from her slumber. "Get up, girl! We got to get ready for Miss Grace's Bible meeting! Now you get up and put on that nice dress I got for you, and have some bread and tea. Abraham and Timothy are already on their way to the chapel, but I told them I would wait for you. Hurry now!"

The rough linen dress scratched her skin as Mara pulled it over her head and fastened it at her waist. The work dress that she had been given to wear to the fields every day was too big, but at least it allowed Mara to move freely, and its worn fabric felt soft against her skin. This dress was newer, and its fabric was scratchy. Its sleeves were too tight, and they stopped just short of her wrists. The bottom of the skirt rested on her ankles, and the clumsy stiff shoes she was told to put on her feet felt strange and uncomfortable.

She gathered her hair into the long braid that Sarah had taught her to make. Mara did not know what the chapel was or why they were going, but it seemed very important to Sarah, and Mara wanted to please her.

"I am ready, Sarah," Mara called out to her. The older woman was waiting outside of the hut, impatiently tapping her foot.

"Come on, Mara! Miss Grace will be starting Bible meeting soon and I do not want to be late."

Linking Mara's arm with hers, Sarah led the way down the dusty path toward a little white clapboard building with a peaked roof and real glass windows on each side. Its large wooden front door was painted red, and it stood open, ready to welcome its Sunday morning worshippers. Sarah and Mara hurried inside, and took their places on the women's side of the room. They sat on roughly hewn benches that were laid out in rows facing the front of the small sanctuary. At the end of the aisle, Miss Grace faced the little congregation.

"Good morning, everyone," Miss Grace said, smiling. "Let us first give thanks to our God for this beautiful day, and for all of the blessings that he has bestowed upon us. Please bow your heads for our morning prayer."

Looking around the room, Mara saw the other slaves close their eyes and turn their faces down toward the plank floor. She did not close her eyes, though. She wanted to see what would happen next. Furtively, Mara raised her face to watch Miss Grace, and was surprised when Miss Grace met her gaze, amusement dancing in her eyes. Apparently she was not angered by the young girl's curiosity, and Mara smiled back at her.

When she finished her prayer, Miss Grace told everyone to sit down in the narrow pews, and she began her reading. She read some stories from a book called the Bible. She read some words about a man named Jesus who wanted everyone to love others more than themselves. Was this Jesus talking about slave owners, too? Mara would have to remember to ask Sarah about that later.

After the reading, the little group sang some songs together about this Jesus, and some of the wonderful things that the Bible told about him. The men and women sang so loudly that the music filled the little building from the crude wood floor to the rough planks of the ceiling. Their songs were happy and comforting, and Mara clapped her hands just like everyone else. It seemed to her that Miss Grace's god was almost as strong and powerful as the Calusa gods, and Mara enjoyed learning about the Christian ways.

At the end of the singing, Miss Grace dismissed the slaves to go back to their houses. Since today was Sunday, the slaves would have the afternoon free to work in their own gardens or to make craft items that they could sell in Charles Town. Sarah was teaching Mara to make the sweet grass baskets that the ladies in town fancied.

As Mara followed Sarah to the door of the chapel, Miss Grace called to them. "Sarah, bring Mara here, please." Miss Grace was standing by a table that held a large pewter bowl filled with water. A towel was placed next to the bowl. "Mara," Miss Grace began, "it is my mother's wish that all of our slaves be baptized into the Christian faith. I would like to do that for you now." Turning to the bowl, she took a small amount of water into her hand, and poured it on top of her head.

"I baptize you in the name of the Father, and of the Son, and of the Holy Spirit," she pronounced solemnly, and then she wiped her hands on the towel. Smiling, Miss Grace continued, "I will also give you the gift of a new name. The pagan name you carry now is not fitting for a Christian girl. From now on, you will be called 'Mary' in honor of our Lord's mother.

"It is a very beautiful and special name. Always remember whose name you bear, and honor her with your thoughts and deeds. You may go now, Mary."

As Mara turned to leave, she was confused. She was to be called Mary? Her mother had given her a name, a much more wonderful and beautiful name. Mara stopped, ready to argue with Miss Grace, but Sarah took her arm and pulled her down the aisle.

"It is all right, child," she said. "I know it is strange, having someone besides your mother giving you a name, but do not fight Miss Grace over this. In your heart you carry your real self and you will not ever let that go.

"Let her call you Mary if she likes. What is that to you? You are Mara of the Calusas. And that will never change."

Although Mara knew the truth of Sarah's words, she wondered if slavery would change her. Would she forget who Mara was and live the rest of her life as the slave Mary? Would she come to care nothing for her freedom or her past? These thoughts were terrible and troubling to Mara.

Fingering the heron that she still wore around my neck, Mara resolved that day to never forget her Calusa gods or her real name.

*How sad it must be to forget who you really are!*

# 14

# A Calusa Atlatl

Though the summer morning had begun soft and cool, wrapped in a shroud of morning mist, the sun had quickly started burning its way through the clouds. Mara knew that by the afternoon great thunderstorms would shatter the quiet of the countryside. She went about her morning chores, fanning herself with palmetto leaves. Perspiration was already pouring from her body, and she yearned for the coolness of the afternoon rains.

Mara still had the distasteful responsibility of emptying the waste buckets every morning for the indigo makers, and she spent each afternoon spreading and drying the indigo leaves in the hot sun. It was late in the day when she finally made her way back to Sarah's hut. Billowing white clouds were forming on the horizon.

"Mama, please!" Timothy begged his mother for permission to accompany Mister Louis down to the riverbank. "It is so much cooler down there, and we will only get a little wet in the river. We will not go any deeper than our knees. I promise, Mama. And if storms come up, we will run home really fast. Please, Mama?"

"Timothy, now you know that some of the men have seen poisonous snakes down there in the marsh, and I worry about you and Mister Louis playing down there all by yourselves. Wait until your father comes home, and maybe he will go down with you. I am sure he would enjoy dipping his tired feet in the nice cool river water."

Timothy was not satisfied with that. "Mama, you know it will almost be dark when he gets home. Besides, Mister Louis wants me to meet him right now. I will be really careful. Please?"

Although Timothy continued to plead, Sarah would not be dissuaded. Finally, Mara volunteered a solution. "Sarah, suppose I take Timothy down to the river? I can keep an eye on him while I collect some herbs for Mistress Stanley. I will be happy to have his company!"

Timothy looked gratefully at Mara, while Sarah considered the suggestion.

"I suppose that will be fine, Mara, if you do not mind. Be very careful, and keep watch. The men said it was a copperhead snake that they saw, and that kind can be very deadly."

Mara promised Sarah that she would be careful, and went to retrieve her gathering sack from the corner of the hut. Thoughtfully, she also picked up the willow stick that she had been carving.

"What is that, Mara? I have noticed you working on it. Is it a spear of some kind?" Timothy turned the strange object over and over in his hands.

"This is an atlatl for hunting, Timothy. My brother Caalus taught me how to use this when I was just a little girl. He was an excellent hunter, and often fed the entire village with the quarry he killed. I think it might be useful to us down at the marsh should we come upon some creature that is not too friendly. Besides, I might be able to use it to put a little extra meat in your Mama's cook pot tonight. Come outside and I will show you how it works."

Curiosity drove Sarah outside with Mara and Timothy to watch the demonstration. Grabbing one of the spears that the slaves used for hunting and fishing, Mara fitted it into the narrow slit that she had carved into the thin, flat willow limb. Holding the atlatl in her left hand Mara drew her arm back as far back as she could. When she flung the atlatl forward, the spear was propelled through the air with amazing speed. It flew well past the other houses in the small slave village, and was lost in the pine forest beyond. Sarah gasped in awe, and Timothy grinned from ear to ear.

"Will you teach me how to do that, Mara?" he asked excitedly.

"When we get down to the marsh where we will not have to fear that someone might be hit by mistake I will let you try. Come on! Let us go now before Mister Louis gets tired of waiting for you!"

Smiling and waving to the tall girl and the little boy, Sarah climbed the steps back into the hut. Mara knew she would busy herself now with preparing dinner for Abraham. He was always famished when he got home.

A little while later as they neared the marsh, Timothy and Mara heard a rustling in the grass, and they knew that Mister Louis had beaten them there.

"Mister Louis!" Timothy cried, "Wait until you see what Mara has made! Show him, Mara!"

"Mara?" Mister Louis looked puzzled. "I was sure your name was 'Mary.' Mother chose that name for you specially! She would be disappointed to think that you did not like it." For once, Mister Louis, whose face usually gleamed with one form of mischief or another, looked very serious.

"Mister Louis, you and your mother and Miss Grace may call me Mary if you wish. But my Calusa name is Mara, and I will never forget that."

Mister Louis simply shrugged his shoulders, and then studied the atlatl that Timothy had handed him. Both boys struggled to position the spear and the atlatl correctly, laughing at each other's clumsiness. Mara left the boys to their playing while she walked through the marsh seeking the plants she needed. Black clouds boiled in the darkening sky, and Mara knew that their time in the marsh would be short.

"Mara! Mara! Come quickly!" she heard Timothy scream from the tidal creek where he and Louis had been playing. Mara heard the fear in his voice, and she knew that something was terribly wrong. Running as fast as she could, Mara made her way through the marsh to the two boys.

"What is it, Timothy? What has happened?" Louis sat on the wet sand. He gripped his left arm, and tried bravely to hold back tears.

"He reached into the grass for the spear, and something bit him, Mara. I am afraid it was the snake Mama had warned me about."

Mara pried Louis' hand from the wound, and sure enough, she could see the small puncture marks that the snake's fangs had made in Mister Louis' soft white skin. Blood dripped from the wound. Mara tore a strip of cloth from the hem of her dress and tied it around Louis' arm to slow the bleeding. Looking along the creek bank Mara spied the snake, crawling among the grasses. It was twice the length of her arm, and brightly colored.

"Timothy, I think that is the snake your Mama described to me. Quickly, get my atlatl and spear," Mara ordered.

Timothy handed Mara her weapon, and she took aim at the snake. She had a good eye, and had been well taught by Caalus. The spear met its mark. Emptying her gathering sack of the herbs and plants, Mara carefully placed the dead snake in the linen pouch.

"We must get you back to the hut as fast as we can," Mara told Louis. "Climb up on my back, and I will carry you." Doing as he was told, Louis held onto her neck with his good arm, and wrapped his legs around her waist. Timothy carefully carried the pouch that contained the snake.

As they hurried home, a terrible storm broke over the plantation. They were soaked to the skin, and terrified about what had just happened to Mister Louis. Sarah saw the fear in their faces, and quickly prepared a resting mat for the boy.

Placing him carefully on the pallet, Mara told Sarah about the snake bite. Mister Louis began to cry then, and even though the terrible storm was raging outside, Timothy ran out of the hut to get Miss Grace.

Pulling the dead snake from her gathering sack Mara said, "Sarah, we have snakes like these at home, but I am not certain what herbs are used to heal the poison bites. Do you know?"

"No, Mara, I have no idea. But that is a copperhead for certain. We will have to rely on your Calusa skill and our faith in God to take care of poor Mister Louis."

Looking at the little boy, Mara could already see signs that the venom was poisoning him. He cried that his arm hurt terribly. When Mara touched his forehead it felt hot, and he complained that his stomach felt sick. He said that everything looked blurry, and that his head felt so light that he thought he might faint.

"The only herb I've ever used for a snake bite is called 'black cohosh,'" Mara told Sarah. "It grows to be about as tall as I am, and is very dark, almost black. Its leaves can be made into a poultice that may cure Mister Louis if I can apply it to the wound quickly. I'll go look for some right now. Brew him some tea from the willow root I have left. That should cool his fever. I will be back as soon as I can."

Through the violent lightning and driving rains, Mara ran to the edge of the fields. Wind whipped at her clothes, and water poured down her face as she struggled to collect the healing cohosh leaves, their sharp edges tearing at her hands as she ripped them from the stems. The lightning, relentless and terrifying, frightened Mara, but she would not return to safety until she had all that she needed. Huge tree branches falling in her path and gusts of wind tearing at her hair and dress made her work nearly impossible. She struggled on, however, determined to get the medicine to cure Mister Louis. Finally, when she had collected what she hoped would be enough, Mara fought her way through the wind and rain back to the hut.

When Mara arrived, soaked to the skin and shivering with cold, Miss Grace was already there. She was kneeling by her brother's side, bathing his forehead with a damp cloth. A half-empty cup of willow tea lay on the floor beside Louis, and Miss Grace was speaking to him in a soothing voice. Louis' eyes were closed, and his breathing was very labored. Mara feared that she might already be too late.

"Mary! Can you help him? Did you find what you need?" The panic in Miss Grace's voice and the terror in her eyes frightened Mara. What would Mister and Mistress Stanley do if she failed to cure their son?

"I can try, Miss Grace. I have never done this before, but I have watched my mother. Sarah, I need your help to prepare this poultice." Quickly, Sarah helped Mara tear up the huge leaves. In just a few minutes, the poultice was applied, and the swelling of the bite seemed to lessen almost instantly.

When Mister Louis opened his eyes sometime later, Mara gave him some of the black cohosh tea that she had prepared. It tasted bitter, but he drank it willingly because he was so thirsty. He complained about pain in his arm, and his stomach still felt sick, but his fever was better and he was not dizzy anymore.

The evening wore on, and the terrible storm abated. Mister Louis fell asleep, breathing easier at last. Abraham lifted the sleeping boy in his strong arms, and carried him back to the main house with Miss Grace close at his heels. Mara had prepared more of the cohosh medicine, and taught Miss Grace the proper way to give it to her little brother. Although Mister Louis seemed better, no one could be certain if he would survive or not. Mara prayed to the faithful Calusa gods that they would spare little Mister Louis.

For the next several days, Mara stayed as close to Louis as she could. She spent her days in the kitchen preparing medicines for Louis and listening to Eve's worried chatter. At night Mara slept in a small storeroom in the cellar. Timothy helped her by doing her daily chores as best he could, and Sarah brought the herbs that Mara needed from the marsh. At night, she often heard Miss Grace praying to her God, asking him to heal her little brother. Mara's prayers to the Calusa gods echoed hers, for even though his family held her freedom from her, he was but a small boy, and Mara did not want him to die. Finally, after many days of waiting, their prayers were answered.

"Mary! Mary!" Miss Grace called one morning, "Come quickly! Louis is hungry! He is hungry! His fever is gone! Come see!"

As she walked into Louis's room, Mara could see that, indeed, he was much better. His eyes were sparkling with health, and he was grinning. His face, which had been pale and gray, was now rosy and bright. Mara smiled at the sight of him.

"Please, Mara, will you bring Timothy to see me?" he asked.

With gratitude in her heart for all of the gods who had heard her prayers, Mara hurried back down to the kitchen to have Eve prepare food for Mister Louis. As she ran down the dirt path to the slave huts, calling Timothy's name, she knew without a doubt that the Calusa gods had bestowed on her the same gift they had granted her mother. Mara was a healer, a true Calusa healer, and she felt very proud.

# Part Three

## *Choices*

# 15

# Jeremiah's Plan

After Bible reading the next Sunday morning, Mara waited for Sarah outside the chapel. The sun was a big ball of orange fire, and she went to the side of the white clapboard building to stand in the shade of a huge magnolia. Mara had loved this tree since the first time she saw it. Its branches bowed low to the ground, and she was nearly hidden by its immense trunk and bright green leaves. It was cool and shadowy here, and the ancient branches not only shaded her from the Carolina sun, but their comforting embrace seemed to shield her from the pain and harshness of her life at Stanley Hall. Mara loved to rub her toes in the lush green moss that grew in the splatters of sunlight and darkness, its softness reminding her of the smooth, cool sand of her home. Mara stole away to this place as often as she could. It was her one and only refuge.

Hidden from view in the shadows, the three men could not see Mara, nor could she see them clearly. They did not know that she was privy to their conversation. They spoke freely, their words of a coming revolution chilling Mara to her very core.

To her surprise, Mara realized that the Stanley's overseer, Stephen, was speaking. "A man named Jeremiah, a slave at Brandon House, is talking about it. I heard him myself saying that he is planning a run-away, and anyone who wants their freedom should meet him at the Amberville Bridge next Sunday. He said to be ready to fight because it is time white folk stopped getting rich off the sweat of black men's backs." The other two men grunted in agreement.

"What is he going to do?" asked a different voice. "How can one man, a Negro at that, end something the white man has laid claim to for years and years?"

"He is planning on killing the plantation owners and their families," the third man stated matter-of-factly. Immediately, Mara recognized Abraham's deep, booming voice.

She listened closely as Abraham continued, "He will be leading an angry gang of men, bent on murdering in the name of freedom. And they will be coming here to Stanley Hall. Master Stanley is one of the richest men in this whole land, and Jeremiah is sure to come after him. His followers have already told all of us here to get our families to safety next Sunday. Since the white men do not carry their weapons on the Lord's Day, Jeremiah figures they will not be armed. He and his men will be able to do what they set out to do without getting hurt."

"Kill Master Stanley and the family? He is a good man, and treats us fair." The second man was indignant.

Stephen continued, "There is nothing fair about one man holding onto the life of another man. No good man, as you say Master Stanley is, would use another man to become wealthy himself. Slavery has got to stop, and since nobody is going to do it for us, I am going to join Jeremiah next Sunday. You are welcome to come, you and anybody else that thirsts for freedom. But if you do not join us, make sure that you and yours are well away from the fighting. There is going to be blood shed, for sure."

Sarah's sudden presence brought the conversation to an abrupt halt. The other two men walked away, leaving Sarah alone with her husband. Sarah's eyes sparkled with the excitement of the good news she was about to share.

"Abraham, I thought Mara was going to wait for me out here. I had to talk to Miss Grace for just a minute. I have the most wonderful news to tell! She wanted to know if we would let Timothy go up to the main house every day when his chores are done so that he can have lessons with Mister Louis. She wants Mara or

'Mary' as she calls her, to come too. She says that Timothy and Mara are both so smart that it would be a shame for them not to read! She says they would both be an even greater help to the plantation if they just had a little education!"

"But, Sarah," Abraham spoke softly and pulled his wife deeper into the shade of the magnolia. "You know that white people are not supposed to be teaching their slaves how to read and write. There is already a law against it. Nobody has been too worried about enforcing it up until now, but we do not want to get Miss Grace into trouble. Besides, what will Mistress Stanley say about all this?"

"She is in favor of it, Abraham! That is the best part! She is so grateful to Mara and Timothy for saving poor Mister Louis from the snakebite, that she has insisted that Miss Grace reward them. Learning to read is the best prize a body, black or white, could win!"

Realizing that he had lost the argument with Sarah, Abraham just shrugged his shoulders and smiled at his wife. "I reckon this is something pretty grand. Mara is going to be real excited when she hears this. Where did she go anyway?"

"I am here," embarrassed to be caught eavesdropping on their conversation, Mara crept sheepishly out from behind the trunk of the tree into the sunlight.

"Mara," Abraham scolded, "You should not be listening to other people's conversations. It is very rude, and you might hear something that you do not want to know." The last few words were said with extra emphasis, for he knew by the fear in Mara's eyes that she had heard him talking about Jeremiah's revolt.

"Oh, what does it matter, Abraham?" Sarah interrupted. "This is such wonderful news that I could not wait to tell her anyway! What do you think, Mara? Would you like to learn to read and write?" Pure joy flooded Mara's face. Although her body would still be enslaved, her mind would be free to learn! Mara knew that she would be able to protect the legacy of her ancestors forever through the words that her hand would learn to write. Her heart was overflowing with gratitude to whatever gods were blessing her with this wonderful opportunity.

Her happiness was brief as her thoughts returned to the conversation she had overheard between Abraham and the two men.

*What will become of Miss Grace and Mister Louis?* Mara wondered. *Should I warn them? But then will I be accused of betraying the people who want to set me free? Will I endanger myself and Abraham, Sarah, and Timothy if I warn the Stanleys of the danger to come?*

As the three slaves walked back to their hut, Mara felt Abraham's eyes studying her. While Sarah bustled about the hut, preparing the midday meal, Abraham pulled Mara aside.

"What will you do with what you have heard, Mara? I do not agree with the killing, for any reason, but I will not stand in the way of the men who are willing to give up their lives for my freedom.

"If you tell of the plan, Mara, these men might kill you as well. This revolution has been building for years, and now it is coming like a terrible tempest. You need to stay far away from its path."

"Is that what you will do, Abraham? Stay out of the storm?"

"Mara, I have to think about Sarah and Timothy. I am going to get them to safety next Sunday. You are part of our family now, and I want you to come with us."

"You are going to let them murder the Stanleys," Mara's voice was flat with despair.

Abraham took her shoulders and turned her toward him. "I want to be free, Mara. I want Timothy to grow up a free man. The Stanleys are about to reap what their ancestors have been sowing for a hundred years. I cannot stop this revolution by myself. All I can do is try to protect my family. If I tell the Stanleys of Jeremiah's plan, I will be killed. My family might be hurt. What else can I do?"

"I must have time to think, Abraham," Mara replied. "No one wants freedom more than I do. But should I allow a life to be taken just so that I might be given back my own?"

With those words, Mara hurried into the house to help Sarah prepare their meal. She needed time to ponder what she had just realized about herself. She was startled by her sudden revelation that a human life, even the life of a slave owner, was more valuable than her own freedom. Would she actually be willing to sacrifice any hope of gaining her freedom in exchange for her master's life?

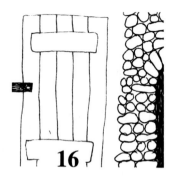

# 16

# A Terrible Tempest

The September morning was cooler and clearer than any day Mara had yet seen in Carolina. There was turmoil in the crisp autumn air however, for today was the day a different kind of tempest would strike. All the slaves knew it was coming. Mara had seen knots of people quietly discussing their plans, only to quickly disband when Miss Grace approached. She overheard whispered warnings and secretive conversations all week. Some of the slaves were readying themselves and their families to flee, while some were preparing to fight. On this day Mara woke early, eager to get her distasteful chore finished while the cool fall breezes hid the stench of the liquid burden she carried. She worked quickly and quietly, wondering what the day would bring. She heard murmurings in the slave quarters as she passed open doors and windows. The people were preparing for the revolt.

Mara did not yet know what she would do. She had not told the Stanleys about the coming danger, but she had not promised to go with Abraham and Sarah either. Her confusion was paralyzing.

Mara was hauling the last of her buckets down the trail toward the indigo house when low voices of men whispering in the trees caused her to stop. Putting the buckets down, she crept through the pine thicket towards the sound. Crouching low, Mara peered through thick bushes. In the dim light of dawn, she could make out the shapes of a dozen men. They were armed with pistols and muskets and angry words.

"Now is the time!" the leader told them, his low voice trembling with rage. Mara knew at once this must be the infamous Jeremiah. "We have waited for this day long enough. Today we will be free. Have courage men, like the courage you showed when we took these weapons this morning. Richardson, that store owner, was a cold, cruel man who didn't care about anything or anyone but himself. He deserved what he got, him and his wife and his daughter. Their deaths will show the other whites that we mean what we say. These weapons we took from his store will serve us well. They will help us shake off the chains of Carolina slavery and begin our new lives of freedom!"

The angry men shouted in agreement, raising their stolen weapons in the air. Mara moved deeper into her hiding place, listening as the man continued.

"Now we are ready to make a stand here at Stanley Hall. Robert Stanley and his fathers have used generations of our people to gain wealth for themselves. Today is their day of reckoning. Be swift in your actions, and show no mercy. Let no man, white or black, stand in your way. Freedom is almost in our hands, but we have to reach out and take it!"

With those words, he motioned for the men to gather around as he began to explain to them his plans for the evil assault.

Terrified, Mara backed out of the thicket, and began to run. *Gods of my fathers,* she prayed silently, *guide me in my steps this day. Show me the way I should go. Find in me the mighty spirit of a great Calusa warrior.*

Ever since Mara had talked with Abraham about Jeremiah's revolt, she had fervently prayed that it would miss Stanley Hall. She had hoped that Miss Grace and Mister Louis would be safe, that Jeremiah and his angry band of rebellious slaves would pass them by. But that prayer had not been answered. Instead, the gods had chosen to test her. And this was her dilemma: if she allows the Stanleys to die, then whatever remains of the honor and pride of the Calusa Indians living in her will die as well; if she helps the Stanleys, then her hope of freedom will be gone forever.

Running as fast as her long legs would allow, Mara made her way toward the main house, and her destiny.

*

Morning light had just begun to sweep across the windows of Stanley Hall. Still wrapped in innocent sleep, the mansion looked impenetrable, solid, and secure.

*Can it withstand the storm that is about to come?* Mara wondered.

Bursting through the kitchen door of Stanley Hall, Mara made her way in the semi-darkness to the main staircase. Climbing the stairs two at a time she reached the landing and began to call Miss Grace's name.

"Miss Grace! Miss Grace!" Mara yelled. One of the white wooden doors along the hall flew open, and Grace rushed toward her.

"Mary, Mary, what is it? What are you doing here? You are not ever supposed to be in the private rooms."

"Miss Grace, please listen. There is not time," Mara spoke haltingly, breathless from both running and terror. "A band of men is coming here to Stanley Hall. They are on the plantation now. They plan to kill you and your family, and they are gathering some of your slaves to help them. Where is Master Stanley?"

"He is away on business. He was called away late last night, and he will not return until tomorrow. What can we do?"

"Quickly, get Mister Louis and Mistress Stanley," Mara answered. "We must hide you before it is too late."

Without a word, Grace did as she was told. Mara helped Mistress Stanley down the long flight of steps to the main floor as Grace followed, carrying a sleepy Louis in her arms.

"Come this way!" Mara pointed to the small door in the corner, the one that hid the steep, narrow staircase used by the house slaves. The steps led to the kitchen below. Moving quickly and silently, Mara shepherded the family into a little storeroom tucked off to the side of a huge fireplace. There, the slave girl hoped her master's family would be safely hidden behind sacks of meal and flour.

"Thank you, Mary," Miss Grace whispered. "I know what helping us must have cost you. Your loyalty will be rewarded."

"I am only doing what I know my Calusa gods would expect of me. Now, be completely silent. I will come for you when the danger has passed. No matter what you hear, do not come out of this room until I return."

Mara squeezed Miss Grace's hand, and slipped out of the room. Behind her she heard Miss Grace bolt the old pine door.

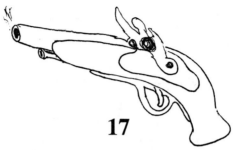

# 17

# Abraham's Choice

Voices screaming in the room upstairs sent Mara flying to the door and out into the light of dawn. Clinging to the ornate banister of the outdoor staircase, she ran as fast as she could to the top. Terrified by what she saw, Mara could only stare. The carved wooden entrance doors had been broken down with an axe, and angry black men were charging through the main hall, throwing over furniture and tearing Miss Grace's beautiful paintings from the walls. The screaming that Mara had heard came from the frightened house maids, who now cowered helplessly in a corner, their hands covering their eyes from the horrible scene.

"Where are they?" one of the men screamed in Mara's face. Shocked, she recognized Stephen, the overseer. He grabbed her arms, and pinned her roughly against the wall. "Where did they go? Did you warn them? You better tell us the truth, girl, or you will pay the price for you lies!"

Staring straight into his eyes, Mara answered as calmly as she could. "At this time of day they should be in their beds sleeping. Where else would they be?" She pushed his hands away from her shoulders, and tried to move past him, but again he grabbed her arm and would not let go.

"Somebody told Jeremiah that an Indian girl named Mary who lived on this plantation overheard some men talking about the plans for this day. He thinks she warned the Stanleys. If she did, she is in more trouble than she knows," he spit the words at Mara angrily. "That girl is you! Am I right? Tell me or I will beat the truth out of you!"

"My name is Mara," she answered honestly. Stephen seemed unconvinced and raised his hand to strike her face.

"Mara!" Abraham yelled as she braced herself for Stephen's fist to strike her cheek. Her assailant turned when he heard the man's voice, then crumpled on the floor at Mara's feet when Abraham's huge fist found its mark on his jaw. Abraham took hold of Mara's arm and pulled her toward the door.

"Come with me!" Abraham hissed as he struggled to lead her down the steps. "I have hidden Sarah and Timothy in a safe place, and there is room for you, too. We must hurry!"

"No, Abraham, no!" Mara cried as she pulled her arm from his grasp. "The Stanleys are hidden here. They are depending on me to protect them. I must tell them when it is safe to come out of hiding. I cannot leave them."

Jeremiah and his band of more than a dozen slaves were ransacking the house. A broom had become a torch in the hands of one angry slave, and the man was moving from room to room lighting anything that would burn. Smoke quickly filled the house. The narrow staircase leading to the kitchen had been discovered, and several of the men were rushing down to search for the Stanleys.

Abraham spoke in Mara's ear. "Where are the Stanleys hiding?"

"In the storeroom by the fireplace. It was the only place I could think of, and now they may be discovered. What can we do?"

Abraham considered for a moment, then replied. "Go down to the kitchen. Listen for the diversion I will provide. Take the Stanleys through the woods to the dock. Move fast and take care that no one sees you. Get them into the boat and down the river away from this place. Go! May your gods and my God guide your steps."

Mara ran back to the kitchen. The men were beating at the door to the store room, and she felt certain that the Stanleys were about to be discovered.

A yell came from upstairs. "Out there, toward the indigo!" Abraham hollered. "Look, there they are! Quick! Get them!" The men stopped pounding on the door, and ran out of the house, hoping to finally trap their human prey. Hiding in the shadows, Mara watched until they were far away, and then cautiously moved to the storeroom.

"Miss Grace! Mistress Stanley! Open the door! We have to move very quickly now!" Slowly the door opened, and the frightened family came out into the kitchen.

Mara continued, "We are going to the dock. We are going to put you in the boat, and get you to a safe place until this all over. Follow me. We are going through the woods so step carefully but quickly! They will realize soon enough that Abraham has tricked them!"

Silently, Mara led her group of refugees from the cellar room, through the lower door and across the broad lawn. "Come, I will help you, Mistress Stanley," Mara said as she gently placed her arm around the older woman's waist to lend support as they crept quickly through the cool grass to the tree line. Miss Grace and Louis followed silently, their eyes wide with terror.

Jeremiah and his angry mob trailed Abraham toward the indigo fields, away from the four figures that were moving stealthily through the trees. Mara could hear the murderous mob's shouts and cries as they searched in vain for the Stanleys.

*When,* Mara wondered, *will they realize that Abraham has deceived them? What will they do to him?*

Moving swiftly through the pine trees that marked the edge of the vast lawn surrounding Stanley Hall, Mara led Mistress Stanley toward the river where a boat was tied to the dock. While Mara untied the boat, Mistress Stanley, Grace, and Louis left the shelter of the pine woods and climbed aboard. Mara pushed the little craft out into the current that would carry them downstream to safety. Lying in the bottom of the boat Miss Grace briefly lifted her head and smiled at Mara. With tears in her eyes she said, "Thank you, Mara." Soon the little boat was carried around a bend, and out of sight.

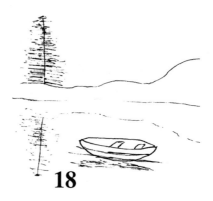

# 18

# An Ending, a Beginning

Once the Stanleys were safely away, Mara's thoughts turned to Abraham. Surely Jeremiah's men had discovered the ruse by now. What must be happening to Abraham?

Mara ran across the wide lawn and down the trail to the indigo house. The men were gathered there, listening as Jeremiah spoke, "We must move on to the next plantation and free our brothers and sisters there," Jeremiah's rage was evident in his voice. Gesturing violently at Abraham, he shouted, "This man helped the Stanleys escape, and so he will pay the price for his deceit. He turned against his own people to aid those who had enslaved him and his family for years. Now, he will suffer the retribution that was intended for the miserable slave owners and their children." The mob cheered in agreement.

Above the yelling of the angry crowd, Mara heard a pistol fire. When the mob stepped back, she saw Abraham lying in a heap on the ground. His legs were drawn up to his chest, and the blood pouring from an open wound in his chest was slowly turning the brown dirt to red mud. Without a backward glance at the man who had just been shot, Jeremiah's gang quickly left through the woods, moving on to the next plantation, eager to kill again.

Tears streamed down Mara's face as she looked at Abraham. She knelt beside him, and placing his head in her lap, she tried to comfort him. Although he was having trouble breathing, he tried to speak to her.

"Mara," he gasped, "Sarah and Timothy will need you. Take care of them. They will rely on your strength." Struggling for each painful breath, he whispered, "Did the Stanleys get away? Did our plan work?"

"Yes, Abraham, yes," Mara said gently, "they are safely down the river. Now please lay quietly and save your strength. Someone will be here soon to help us."

"No, Mara, there is no time. Promise me," he grabbed her hand then as his voice trailed off. He looked pleadingly into Mara's face.

"You have been a brother to me, Abraham. I will do what you ask." As Mara watched Abraham's face, the light of life left his eyes, the breath left his body, and he was gone.

*

Jeremiah's rebellion was short-lived. Later that same day, a group of white planters caught up with Jeremiah and his men. When the gunfire was over, all of the rebellious slaves and several plantation owners were dead. The September morning that had dawned with all the hope and beauty of an early autumn day ended with a bitter cold rain that rinsed away the blood of slain men, black and white, slave and free.

*

Abraham's funeral was held in the small slave cemetery on Stanley plantation. Miss Grace read passages from the Bible, and Mister Louis covered the wooden coffin with flowers. Many people came to the service to honor Abraham, for they had heard the story of his brave sacrifice. As everyone lifted their voices to sing the Christian hymns that Abraham had loved, Mara was reminded once again of the Calusa women and the songs they sang to praise their gods. These memories were not as painful as they had once been, for now she knew that she had found a new home. She yearned for the freedom of her Calusa childhood, but she would always honor her promise to Abraham. The love that Mara felt for Sarah and Timothy bound her heart to this place in a way that chains never could.

After the funeral, Miss Grace walked back to the slave quarters with Sarah, Timothy, and Mara.

"Sarah," Miss Grace began, "Abraham was one of the bravest men I have ever met. I would like to honor his memory by offering you and your son the freedom he refused to take through violence."

Turning to Mara, Miss Grace continued, "I offer this same reward to you, Mary. Even though your freedom was stolen from you in a cruel and terrible way, you have demonstrated your loyalty and bravery time and time again. I can never return to you all that you have lost, but I offer to you what I have. Please let me teach you to read and write so that you may be free not only in body, but in mind and spirit as well." Mara stood silently, waiting for Miss Grace to finish.

"There is a small cottage on the grounds near the main house that was once used by a caretaker. I offer this to you, Sarah, as your new home, so that I may be close to Mary and Timothy for our daily reading lessons. If you prefer, though, you may leave Stanley Hall. I am aware of a small community of freed Africans on Sullivans Island, and I am sure that they would welcome you."

Sarah looked into Miss Grace's eyes, tears filling her own. "Why would I want to leave, Miss Grace? My Abraham is here, and here is where I will stay. Someday soon, though, my son will take the reward that you offer. He will honor the memory of his father by claiming his freedom, and he will use it to gain the freedom of more of our people. Not through violence like Jeremiah, but with peace and understanding. Someday, I pray, good people will rise up, and put an end to slavery altogether."

Sarah turned away from Grace, and clutching her son's small hand, she walked back to the hut she had shared with her husband for so many years. Their lives had been changed forever by the hatred and greed that could only be found inside the human heart.

# Epilogue

*Stanley Hall, Circa 1800*

Mara did not again taste the salty air of her home,
nor did she feel its soft sand beneath her feet.
She did not again see the diving pelicans,
nor watch as an arribada of turtles
journeyed to Calusa shores.

She did not see her mother again,
or Caalus, or little Lupa,
and she never knew what became of her people,
for long ago the mighty Calusa vanished.
Some, like Mara, were sold into slavery,
others died of the vicious diseases that were brought to the land
by the Europeans.
And others simply disappeared.

In the years that followed Jeremiah's Rebellion,
Mara became a wife, a mother, and a grandmother.
She never left Sarah,
though Timothy left when he became a man.
His search for freedom took him far away from Stanley Hall
and its indigo fields
to the rolling hills and factories of the North.
There he fought with those of like mind,
the Abolitionists, both black and white,
who believed in freedom for all.
His weapons were not pistols, but words.
Even now, Mara can feel his father's pride.

During her years spent at Stanley Hall
Mara came to share some of the Christian beliefs
of the slaves with whom she lived,
for at times she found comfort
in the songs that they sang in the fields as they worked,
and in the words of their great god.
But still in her heart and soul,
Mara held tightly to the gods of her people.
She could not, would not
forsake them.
She taught the new generation the ways of their ancestors
and in her writings she recorded the traditions of her people.
In these ways Mara honored the memory
of the mighty Calusa.

Her body does not lie in a sacred shell mound
made by her people, the Shell People.
Nor does it rest in a watery tomb
where those who are evil are buried
so that their spirits can no longer bother the living.

Instead, Mara's bones rest in a shaded grave
marked with an ancient stone now rubbed smooth
by the Carolina winds and rains.
It is just like many other graves
found in the slave cemetery at Stanley Hall.

Around her neck, even in death,
hangs the heron that Caalus carved for her
in a long ago place,
in a long ago time.

Mara sleeps quietly next to others like her,
poor souls stolen from their homes and families
to serve the needs of the greedy and powerful.

If someday you should stumble upon Mara's resting place,
do not be afraid.
Ask her questions, and she will share her wisdom with you,
for her soul could not be
plundered by pirates,
or crushed by cruel masters.

Her spirit remains with her,
ever alive,
deep within her eyes,
the eyes of the Calusa.

# Glossary

**Arribada**—a mass nesting of sea turtles, sometimes involving more than 200 of the animals coming to shore at one time

**Atlatl**— a lever-like tool carved from wood that is used by hunters to enable a spear to fly with more force and power

**Booty**—the treasure a pirate accumulated by stealing

**Cacique**—the ruler or king of the Calusa tribe

**Calusa**—This fierce tribe of Native Americans, also known as the Shell People, lived in Southwest Florida beginning before 500 A.D. At the height of their civilization, the Calusa controlled the entire southern half of Florida. They navigated through their empire by canoe, traveling the extensive canal system they constructed. The appearance of European explorers who brought new diseases is largely responsible for the decline of the Calusa civilization. The Calusa had completely disappeared from Florida by 1750.

**Carapace**—the upper shell of a turtle

**Careen**—to beach a ship on shore in order to expose its hull; crew members careened a ship in order to scrape off barnacles and other sea life that had attached themselves to the bottom of a ship during long voyages

**Cassina**—a species of holly plant used by Native Americans to make a popular medicine called "the black drink"; Indian healers brewed the plant leaves into a strong tea.

**Coffle**—a group of captives being transported to a slave market for sale at auction

**Forecastle**—(foke-s'l) the upper deck of the ship in front of the foremast

**Frigate**—a fast, medium-sized sailing ship favored by pirates during the eighteenth century

**Indigo**—known as the "King of Dyestuffs," indigo is a blue dye that was made solely from plants until the late nineteenth century

**Jolly Boat**—a small boat used by a ship's crew for general work and transportation

**Mahoma**—the name used by the Calusa Indians for the temple where their religious ceremonies were conducted

**Marooning**—punishing a pirate by leaving him on an isolated island where he was forced to survive alone

**Plastron**—bony plate forming the underside of a turtle's shell

**Quartermaster**—an elected officer on a pirate ship who was in charge of distributing supplies

**Shaman**—the religious leader of the Calusa Indians, a shaman conducted ceremonies in the Mahoma and prepared the sacrifices offered in fires burned on top of the shell mound

# Author's Notes

Some things in this book are real, and others are part of an author's imagination. This section will help you understand the difference.

Although Mara did not exist, the Calusa Indians were real. They were fierce warriors who were ruling the southwest region of Florida when the European explorers, like Juan Ponce de Leon, arrived in the 1500s. Sometimes called the Shell People, the Calusas built their houses and important buildings on mounds called middens made from seashells and soil.

The Calusas ate many different kinds of shellfish, crabs, turtles, and fish. An arribada of sea turtles as described in the early chapters of this book would have brought much excitement to the village because of the food and resources the turtles provided. Today sea turtles are endangered. It is against the law to hunt turtles or to dig up their eggs. If you happen to see a turtle nest, do not disturb it. Instead, notify the authorities in the area so that the nest can be marked and protected.

The Calusa used seashells as tools for hunting, harvesting, building, and artwork. It is possible that the amulet given to Mara by her brother Caluus would have been carved from pine or red cedar wood. Hunting for food was done with spears, atlatls, and nets. The Calusas gathered plants such as hogplum, sea grape, and cocoplum to use for food and medicine.

By the middle of the eighteenth century the Calusa Indians had almost completely disappeared from Florida. Many died from diseases such as typhus and smallpox which were brought to the region by the European explorers. Some were killed by other Native American tribes and some Calusas, like Mara, were sold into slavery. A few may have escaped to Cuba, but there are no historical records of Calusa villages or towns existing anywhere in Florida at the end of the 1700s.

Hannah Dunne and Grace Stanley are also fictional. However, these characters are based on people that did exist during the eighteenth century. For example, fictional indigo planter Grace Stanley was inspired by the real Eliza Lucas Pinckney who lived in South Carolina and began running her father's plantation when she was only a teenager. Eliza taught her sister and two black children to read, and she did study art. She is best remembered for developing the method of processing indigo that was widely used in South Carolina and which provided a great source of income for her family and other planters in the area. The method described in this book for making indigo cakes is the process that was used by the slaves on the plantations.

Captain Hannah Dunne's character was modeled after two female pirates who lived in the early 1700s. Mary Read and Anne Bonny reportedly sailed throughout the Caribbean Sea with pirate Calico Jack Rachham. Although women were not usually permitted on board pirate ships, these two supposedly disguised themselves as men and sailed along with Calico Jack's crew. They fought as fiercely as the men, and were eventually arrested and imprisoned in Jamaica. The rest of the crew, including Captain Jack himself, was tried for piracy, convicted, and sentenced to death.

There exists little information about the early life of Edward Teach, known as the pirate Blackbeard. The rhyme Mara learned on board the *Devil Ray* was a song Blackbeard's crew sang in taverns on shore to attract young men to serve aboard their ship, the *Queen Anne's Revenge*. Probably one of the best-known pirates, Edward Teach's nickname came from the long black beard that he braided and tied with ribbons. Legend says that Blackbeard would insert slow-burning cords under his hat, causing rings of smoke to circle his head, giving him a very devilish and frightening appearance. Blackbeard was killed in a battle near the coast of North Carolina in November 1718. The commander of the opposing ship, Lieutenant Robert Maynard of the Royal Navy, cut off Teach's head, and hung it at as trophy from the bowsprit of his ship. Far from the Carolina coast, Blackbeard's death was the subject of an article printed in the Boston Newsletter, written by a young Ben Franklin:

> *Have you heard of Teach the Rover, and his Knavery on the Main;*
> *How of Gold he was a Lover, how he lov'd all ill got gain . . ."*

It has been suggested that some pirate ships were run like small democracies with the pirates themselves making the important decisions that affected the entire crew. If this is true, crew members who had been loyal to Captain Dunne's father could have voted to allow Hannah to remain as captain of the *Devil Ray*. It is reported that pirates did capture Native Americans living in the region of Southwest Florida in order to sell them at the slave markets in Charleston, South Carolina. This would have been a very lucrative business for pirates during that time period.

Likewise, crew members could have been responsible for choosing the fictional Mr. Leon's fate of marooning. In attempting to drown Mara, he was actually stealing from his shipmates. That disloyal action would have required severe punishment, and marooning would have been the most likely action taken. "Walking the plank" did not exist.

Research has found that some Africans who had been captured in order to be sold in the slave markets were given the opportunity to choose between life as a pirate or life as a slave. It is possible that one such African would be aboard ship with Mara. In this story, the African's name is Samuel.

Many resources were used in the writing of this book. Additional information about pirates, plantations, and slavery may be found in the following books: *Pirates of the Southern Coast* by

Sandra MacLean Clunies and Bruce Roberts; *Historic Communities: Life on a Plantation* by Bobbie Kalman; and *Indigo in America* published by the Charles Towne Landing Foundation, Charleston, South Carolina. For more information about the Calusas, read *The Calusa and Their Legacy: South Florida and Their Environments* by Darcie A. MacMahon and William H. Marquardt or *The Crafts of Florida's First People* by Robin C. Brown.

# About the Author

Holly Moulder taught elementary school in Newnan, Georgia, for twenty-one years. She has combined her love of literature and history to create her first novel, *Eyes of the Calusa*. She lives in Sharpsburg, Georgia, with her husband Don and daughter Lauren.

# About the Illustrator

Teri Wilson holds a degree in interior design from Bauder College and has applied her artistic talents to set and costume design. This is her first children's book. She lives in Stockbridge, Georgia, with her husband Dave.

CPSIA information can be obtained at www.ICGtesting.com
Printed in the USA
LVOW07s2034271115

464357LV00020B/127/P